Your Path to Financial Literacy, Wealth-Building and Wellbeing

Money TALK$

FINANCIAL WELLBEING PLANNER

A multi-sensory financial planner designed to educate, empower, inspire, and transform your journey to self-discovery and enhanced wellbeing.

DR. CONSTANCE CRAIG-MASON, MRFC®, NSSA®

FINANCIAL WELLBEING PLANNER

Money TALK$™ Financial Wellbeing Planner
Author: Dr. Constance Craig-Mason, MRFC®, NSSA®

Editor & Publisher: Pierucci Publishing LLC
P.O. Box 2074, Carbondale, Colorado 81623, USA
www.pieruccipublishing.com
Tel: (855)720-1111

Copyright Owner: Concierge Financial Advisory, LLC
York, Pennsylvania, USA

Cover design by SDP Business Studio
Edited by Pierucci Publishing

Coloring Page Illustrations by Princella Seripenah

For inquiries, please contact:
Concierge Financial Advisory, LLC
1003 N. George Street, Suite #1
York, PA 17404
Email: constance@conciergefg.com

Spiral Bound ISBN: 978-1-962578-88-2
Paperback ISBN: 978-1-962578-61-5
Ebook ISBN: 978-1-962578-62-2
Library of Congress Control Number: 2025906513

This planner belongs to:

YOUR FULL NAME:

If found, please contact me at:

TELEPHONE:

EMAIL ADDRESS:

2025

January

Su	Mo	Tu	We	Th	Fr	Sa
				1	2	3
4	5	6	7	8	9	10
11	12	13	14	15	16	17
18	19	20	21	22	23	24
25	26	27	28	29	30	31

February

Su	Mo	Tu	We	Th	Fr	Sa
1	2	3	4	5	6	7
8	9	10	11	12	13	14
15	16	17	18	19	20	21
22	23	24	25	26	27	28

March

Su	Mo	Tu	We	Th	Fr	Sa
						1
2	3	4	5	6	7	8
9	10	11	12	13	14	15
16	17	18	19	20	21	22
23	24	25	26	27	28	29
30	31					

April

Su	Mo	Tu	We	Th	Fr	Sa
		1	2	3	4	5
6	7	8	9	10	11	12
13	14	15	16	17	18	19
20	21	22	23	24	25	26
27	28	29	30			

May

Su	Mo	Tu	We	Th	Fr	Sa
					1	2
3	4	5	6	7	8	9
10	11	12	13	14	15	16
17	18	19	20	21	22	23
24	25	26	27	28	29	30
31						

June

Su	Mo	Tu	We	Th	Fr	Sa
	1	2	3	4	5	6
7	8	9	10	11	12	13
14	15	16	17	18	19	20
21	22	23	24	25	26	27
28	29	30				

July

Su	Mo	Tu	We	Th	Fr	Sa
		1	2	3	4	5
6	7	8	9	10	11	12
13	14	15	16	17	18	19
20	21	22	23	24	25	26
27	28	29	30	31		

August

Su	Mo	Tu	We	Th	Fr	Sa
					1	2
3	4	5	6	7	8	9
10	11	12	13	14	15	16
17	18	19	20	21	22	23
24	25	26	27	28	29	30
31						

September

Su	Mo	Tu	We	Th	Fr	Sa
		1	2	3	4	5
6	7	8	9	10	11	12
13	14	15	16	17	18	19
20	21	22	23	24	25	26
27	28	29	30			

October

Su	Mo	Tu	We	Th	Fr	Sa
				1	2	3
4	5	6	7	8	9	10
11	12	13	14	15	16	17
18	19	20	21	22	23	24
25	26	27	28	29	30	31

November

Su	Mo	Tu	We	Th	Fr	Sa
						1
2	3	4	5	6	7	8
9	10	11	12	13	14	15
16	17	18	19	20	21	22
23	24	25	26	27	28	29
30						

December

Su	Mo	Tu	We	Th	Fr	Sa
	1	2	3	4	5	6
7	8	9	10	11	12	13
14	15	16	17	18	19	20
21	22	23	24	25	26	27
28	29	30	31			

2026

January

Su	Mo	Tu	We	Th	Fr	Sa
				1	2	3
4	5	6	7	8	9	10
11	12	13	14	15	16	17
18	19	20	21	22	23	24
25	26	27	28	29	30	31

February

Su	Mo	Tu	We	Th	Fr	Sa
1	2	3	4	5	6	7
8	9	10	11	12	13	14
15	16	17	18	19	20	21
22	23	24	25	26	27	28

March

Su	Mo	Tu	We	Th	Fr	Sa
1	2	3	4	5	6	7
8	9	10	11	12	13	14
15	16	17	18	19	20	21
22	23	24	25	26	27	28
29	30	31				

April

Su	Mo	Tu	We	Th	Fr	Sa
			1	2	3	4
5	6	7	8	9	10	11
12	13	14	15	16	17	18
19	20	21	22	23	24	25
26	27	28	29	30		

May

Su	Mo	Tu	We	Th	Fr	Sa
					1	2
3	4	5	6	7	8	9
10	11	12	13	14	15	16
17	18	19	20	21	22	23
24	25	26	27	28	29	30
31						

June

Su	Mo	Tu	We	Th	Fr	Sa
	1	2	3	4	5	6
7	8	9	10	11	12	13
14	15	16	17	18	19	20
21	22	23	24	25	26	27
28	29	30				

July

Su	Mo	Tu	We	Th	Fr	Sa
			1	2	3	4
5	6	7	8	9	10	11
12	13	14	15	16	17	18
19	20	21	22	23	24	25
26	27	28	29	30	31	

August

Su	Mo	Tu	We	Th	Fr	Sa
						1
2	3	4	5	6	7	8
9	10	11	12	13	14	15
16	17	18	19	20	21	22
23	24	25	26	27	28	29
30	31					

September

Su	Mo	Tu	We	Th	Fr	Sa
		1	2	3	4	5
6	7	8	9	10	11	12
13	14	15	16	17	18	19
20	21	22	23	24	25	26
27	28	29	30			

October

Su	Mo	Tu	We	Th	Fr	Sa
				1	2	3
4	5	6	7	8	9	10
11	12	13	14	15	16	17
18	19	20	21	22	23	24
25	26	27	28	29	30	31

November

Su	Mo	Tu	We	Th	Fr	Sa
1	2	3	4	5	6	7
8	9	10	11	12	13	14
15	16	17	18	19	20	21
22	23	24	25	26	27	28
29	30					

December

Su	Mo	Tu	We	Th	Fr	Sa
		1	2	3	4	5
6	7	8	9	10	11	12
13	14	15	16	17	18	19
20	21	22	23	24	25	26
27	28	29	30	31		

2027

January

Su	Mo	Tu	We	Th	Fr	Sa
					1	2
3	4	5	6	7	8	9
10	11	12	13	14	15	16
17	18	19	20	21	22	23
24	25	26	27	28	29	30
31						

February

Su	Mo	Tu	We	Th	Fr	Sa
	1	2	3	4	5	6
7	8	9	10	11	12	13
14	15	16	17	18	19	20
21	22	23	24	25	26	27
28						

March

Su	Mo	Tu	We	Th	Fr	Sa
	1	2	3	4	5	6
7	8	9	10	11	12	13
14	15	16	17	18	19	20
21	22	23	24	25	26	27
28	29	30	31			

April

Su	Mo	Tu	We	Th	Fr	Sa
				1	2	3
4	5	6	7	8	9	10
11	12	13	14	15	16	17
18	19	20	21	22	23	24
25	26	27	28	29	30	

May

Su	Mo	Tu	We	Th	Fr	Sa
						1
2	3	4	5	6	7	8
9	10	11	12	13	14	15
16	17	18	19	20	21	22
23	24	25	26	27	28	29
30	31					

June

Su	Mo	Tu	We	Th	Fr	Sa
		1	2	3	4	5
6	7	8	9	10	11	12
13	14	15	16	17	18	19
20	21	22	23	24	25	26
27	28	29	30			

July

Su	Mo	Tu	We	Th	Fr	Sa
				1	2	3
4	5	6	7	8	9	10
11	12	13	14	15	16	17
18	19	20	21	22	23	24
25	26	27	28	29	30	31

August

Su	Mo	Tu	We	Th	Fr	Sa
1	2	3	4	5	6	7
8	9	10	11	12	13	14
15	16	17	18	19	20	21
22	23	24	25	26	27	28
29	30	31				

September

Su	Mo	Tu	We	Th	Fr	Sa
			1	2	3	4
5	6	7	8	9	10	11
12	13	14	15	16	17	18
19	20	21	22	23	24	25
26	27	28	29	30		

October

Su	Mo	Tu	We	Th	Fr	Sa
					1	2
3	4	5	6	7	8	9
10	11	12	13	14	15	16
17	18	19	20	21	22	23
24	25	26	27	28	29	30
31						

November

Su	Mo	Tu	We	Th	Fr	Sa
	1	2	3	4	5	6
7	8	9	10	11	12	13
14	15	16	17	18	19	20
21	22	23	24	25	26	27
28	29	30				

December

Su	Mo	Tu	We	Th	Fr	Sa
			1	2	3	4
5	6	7	8	9	10	11
12	13	14	15	16	17	18
19	20	21	22	23	24	25
26	27	28	29	30	31	

About the Money TALK$™ Movement

Born in 2020 from the chaos and uncertainty of the COVID-19 pandemic, the Money TALK$ Movement is a beacon of hope, resilience, and transformation. Spearheaded by Dr. Constance Craig-Mason, "Money TALK$™ Volume I" and "Money TALK$™ Volume II" became a powerful platform wherein thirty-six P.O.W.E.R. couple co-authors shared their unfiltered truths, struggles, and triumphs. Together, the authors revealed how they weathered the storms of love, money, and entrepreneurship while navigating work-life balance during one of the most challenging times in modern history.

By 2023, the world was still grappling with the residual effects of the pandemic—emotionally, mentally, and financially. In response, the release of "Money TALK$ Volume III" elevated the movement to new heights. Featuring a foreword by legendary motivational speaker Dr. Les Brown and contributions from twenty-four African American financial thought-leaders worldwide, this collective effort brought financial literacy to the forefront, empowering historically underserved communities to embrace financial independence.

But the Money TALK$™ Movement is more than just a series of books; it's a catalyst for change and the cornerstone of a larger mission. With its three-part financial empowerment tool kit, the movement offers an interactive, multi-sensory experience combining financial education with emotional and mental wellbeing. This transformative resource guides individuals on their journey to self-discovery and financial empowerment, fostering resilience and clarity along the way.

Additionally, the Money TALK$™ Movement extends its reach through the "Money TALK$™: Wealth Beyond Numbers" podcast, providing ongoing inspiration and practical strategies from experts worldwide. It also invites everyone to join the exclusive Wealth & Wellness Collective, an empowering community dedicated to continuous learning, growth, and support.

At its core, the Money TALK$™ Movement normalizes transformative conversations about money, providing a safe space to rewrite financial narratives. Driven by real entrepreneurs sharing real experiences, it pulls back the curtain on "how money works."

Dr. Constance's belief is clear: *"Wealth isn't just what you hold—it's what you heal."* Join the Money TALK$™ Movement in healing what no longer serves you. True generational wealth is built when we rewrite the narratives we've inherited.

"PLAN, BE, LIVE WELL... without worrying about money!"

How to Navigate the Money TALK$™ Financial Wellbeing Planner

Welcome to the Money TALK$™ Financial Wellbeing Planner, your partner in creating financial stability, independence, and confidence. This isn't just a planner; it's a multi-sensory journey designed to transform the way you think about and manage money. Whether you're starting fresh, tackling debt, or working toward wealth-building, this planner will meet you where you are, providing practical tools, reflective prompts, and empowering insights to help you build the life you deserve—without worrying about money. Here's how to navigate each section and make it work for you:

SECTION ONE

Introduction & Financial Wellbeing: Kick things off by exploring what financial wellbeing means for you. This section helps you understand how your money choices connect to your values, goals, and dreams.

Action: Reflect on your current financial situation and set intentions for how you'll use this planner to create the financial life you want.

SECTION TWO

Overcoming Financial Trauma: We all carry money stories from the past that shape our present habits. This section invites you to reflect on those stories and rewrite the ones holding you back.

Action: Use the journaling prompts to explore how your past has influenced your financial mindset and identify steps to break free from limiting beliefs.

SECTION THREE

Financial Literacy & Education: Knowledge is power! Learn the basics of personal finance—broken down into simple, easy-to-understand concepts that build your confidence.

Action: Dive into the financial terms and examples, then test your knowledge with the quiz. Make notes on areas you'd like to strengthen.

How to Navigate the Money TALK$™ Financial Wellbeing Planner

SECTION FOUR

Monthly Tracking & Review - The 50-30-20 Rule: Progress is powerful. This section helps you track your income, expenses, and savings each month to see how far you've come.

Action: Review your spending plan regularly. Adjust where needed and celebrate even the smallest wins.

SECTION FIVE

Spending Plan Creation: Forget "budgeting." This is about putting you in the driver's seat with a Spending Plan that aligns with your goals, dreams, and values.

Action: Use the templates to design a plan that gives every dollar a purpose while leaving room for flexibility and grace.

SECTION SIX

Debt Payoff Acceleration: Debt doesn't define you. This section equips you with strategies like the "snowball" or "avalanche" methods to pay down debt and reclaim your financial freedom.

Action: Organize your debts with the tracking templates and stay motivated by celebrating milestones along the way.

SECTION SEVEN

Savings Challenge: Saving doesn't have to be boring. With interactive challenges, you'll build your savings in a way that's fun and rewarding.

Action: Join the 52-week Savings Challenge and use the **Paycheck Power Booster.**

How to Navigate the Money TALK$™ Financial Wellbeing Planner

SECTION EIGHT

Growing Assets: Your money should work as hard as you do. This section shows you how to grow your assets and set the foundation for long-term wealth.

Action: List your current assets, identify opportunities for growth, and create an action plan for building wealth.

SECTION NINE

Leveraging Assets: Assets can do more than sit idle—they can create opportunities. Learn how to use what you already have to open new doors and grow your wealth.

Action: Develop a plan to leverage assets like investments, property, or skills to generate additional income.

SECTION TEN

Protecting Assets: Building wealth is just the first step; protecting it is the key to sustaining it. Learn how to safeguard your assets through smart strategies.

Action: Review the checklist and create a plan for insurance, estate planning, and risk management.

How to Navigate the Money TALK$™ Financial Wellbeing Planner

SECTION ELEVEN

Financial Concepts Cheatsheets: Master foundational concepts that simplify personal finance and help you make informed decisions with confidence.

Topics include:

- The Wealth Formula
- The Rule of 72 (Compound Interest)
- Dollar Cost Averaging
- Investment Decision Filter
- Sequence of Returns Risk
- The 3-Legged Stool (Redesigned for today)
- The Bucket Plan

Action: Use these frameworks to guide discussions with your advisor or to create a strategy tailored to your goals.

SECTION TWELVE

Small Business Spending Plan & Tracking (Bonus Section): If you're an entrepreneur, this section helps you manage your business finances and reinvest for growth.

Action: Track income, expenses, and profits. Use the templates to create a sustainable business plan.

Tips for Success

1. **Stay Consistent:** Set aside time each week to engage with your planner. Reflection is key to progress.
2. **Be Honest:** This is your safe space to acknowledge challenges and celebrate growth.
3. **Set SMART Goals:** Specific, Measurable, Achievable, Relevant, and Time-bound goals keep you motivated.
4. **Celebrate Progress:** Every small step forward is a win. Give yourself credit and keep building!

With the **Money TALK$™ Financial Wellbeing Planner**, you're not just managing money—you're creating a legacy, healing what no longer serves you, and unlocking the confidence to live life on your terms. **Let's rewrite your financial story together.**

Money TALK$

INTRODUCTION + FINANCIAL WELLBEING

Scan for a FREE episode about Transforming Your Money Mindset

SECTION ONE

MONTHLY PLANNER

MONTH & YEAR

SUN	MON	TUE	WED	THU	FRI	SAT

TO DO:

THIS MONTH'S GOALS

MONTHLY AFFIRMATIONS

POSITIVE AFFIRMATION

Neuroscientists agree that without belief, you will not be capable of rewriring your brain for abundance and prosperity. Please repeat this affirmation at regular intervals throughout your day every day this month.

I AM
capable of creating the life I desire.

Money TALKS

THE PURPOSE OF THE PLANNER

Welcome to the Money TALK$™ Financial Wellbeing Planner—a transformative tool for redefining your relationship with money. This isn't just another planner; it's a multi-sensory experience created to guide you on a journey toward emotional, mental, and financial freedom.

We understand that money is deeply personal. It's not just numbers on a page—it's tied to your dreams, challenges, and the life you want to live. That's why this planner is designed to meet you where you are. It's here to help you reclaim control, build confidence, and align your financial decisions with your values.

Whether you're tackling debt, navigating life's unexpected "what ifs," or building generational wealth, this planner is your roadmap to financial wellbeing. It's filled with reflective exercises, actionable steps, and creative tools that turn financial planning into a journey of self-discovery and empowerment.

FINANCIAL WELLBEING

Financial wellbeing isn't just about having more money; it's about living a life where your finances serve you—not the other way around. Inspired by the Consumer Financial Protection Bureau (CFPB) framework, true financial wellbeing means:

- Feeling in control of your finances—day to day, month to month.
- Having the ability to handle life's surprises without unraveling.
- Staying on track with your goals and dreams.
- Having the financial freedom to make choices that bring you joy and peace.

But let's take it a step further: financial wellbeing is also about **healing past money wounds**, breaking generational cycles, and creating a future that reflects your worth and purpose.

WHY FINANCIAL WELLBEING IS ESSENTIAL FOR SUCCESS

When you're financially secure, your world shifts. You can breathe easier, focus on what matters most, and move through life with **clarity, resilience, and confidence.** Financial wellbeing is the foundation for not just wealth, but **health, happiness, and freedom.**

Without financial wellbeing, financial stress can feel like a heavy weight. It creeps into every corner of your life—your health, relationships, and opportunities. But with the right tools, you can take that weight off your shoulders and step into a life of balance and possibility.

Money TALK$ FACT

Based on a 2024 study, Bankrate® reported that only **25%** (1 in 4) Americans stated they were financially secure.

This declined from 28% in the 2023 study.

Source: https://www.bankrate.com/banking/financial-freedom-survey

That's what this planner is all about. It's here to help you:

- **Get crystal clear** on your financial starting point.
- **Align your money with your life's purpose and goals.**
- **Create a spending plan** that gives every dollar a job and reflects what matters most to you.
- **Build a safety net** so you can handle life's twists and turns with grace.
- **Plan for the future** with confidence, so you're always one step ahead.

With the **Money TALK$™ Financial Wellbeing Planner**, you're not just managing money—you're **reclaiming power, rewriting narratives, and designing a life you love.**

JOURNAL ENTRY

Date:

When you think about your financial wellbeing, what does success look like to you?

How does that vision align with your current reality, and what steps do you think you need to take to close the gap?

"The only limit to our realization of tomorrow is our doubts of today."
— Franklin D. Roosevelt

CREATE YOUR VISION
OF FINANCIAL WELLBEING

Understanding your financial wellbeing is crucial to achieving your personal and professional goals. To begin this journey, it's important to have a clear vision of what financial wellbeing looks like for you. We're here to give you the space and tools you need to create your financial wellbeing vision board, a powerful visual representation of your financial goals and dreams. This board will serve as a constant reminder of what you're working towards, keeping you motivated and focused on your path to financial success.

Here's what our friends at www.medium.com suggest a vision board may look like!

A vision board is a collection of images, words, and other visual elements that represent your financial goals and aspirations. To create one, start by reflecting on what financial wellbeing means to you. Gather magazines, print out pictures, and find quotes that resonate with your financial dreams-whether it's saving for a home, eliminating debt, or achieving a certain lifestyle. Arrange these elements on a board or a large piece of paper, and place it somewhere you'll see it daily. This daily visual cue will help keep your goals top of mind and inspire you to take the necessary steps to achieve them.

CREATE YOUR VISION
BOARD HERE

CREATE YOUR VISION
BOARD HERE

MONTHLY RECAP

MONTH OF

THIS MONTH'S ACHIEVEMENTS

WHAT DO YOU FEEL WORKED THIS MONTH?

WHAT DO YOU FEEL DIDN'T WORK THIS MONTH?

THINGS TO DO MORE OF

MONTHLY GRATITUDE

Money
TALK$

OVERCOMING FINANCIAL TRAUMA

Scan for a FREE EPISODE: From Trauma to Triumph!

SECTION TWO

MONTHLY PLANNER

MONTH & YEAR

SUN	MON	TUE	WED	THU	FRI	SAT

TO DO:

THIS MONTH'S GOALS

MONTHLY AFFIRMATIONS

POSITIVE AFFIRMATION

I MAKE intentional choices that support my goals.

Money TALK$

WHAT IS "FINANCIAL TRAUMA"?

"Financial trauma" refers to the psychological distress and emotional pain caused by significant financial hardship or instability. This can result from events like job loss, mounting debt, unexpected expenses, or economic downturns. It often leads to chronic stress, anxiety, feelings of shame, and can negatively impact mental health and overall wellbeing. The experience of financial trauma can also affect one's relationship with money and financial decision-making long-term.

Money TALK$ FACT

A staggering **68%** of U.S. adults feel they have suffered from, or are currently suffering from, **financial trauma** according to new research released by Experian® in 2023.

Source: https://www.experianplc.com/newsroom/press-releases/2023

In this section, you will find exercises designed to help you identify and release limiting beliefs while addressing financial trauma. These exercises encourage deep reflection and provide practical steps for breaking free from negative financial patterns. By engaging with these activities, you will be able to rebuild a positive mindset and take empowered action toward your financial goals.

Take your time completing each exercise with vulnerability and honesty for the best results. Reflecting back through journaling after each exercise will further enhance your progress. Approach each task with an open heart, allowing yourself to fully engage in the process of transformation.

Identify Your Limiting Beliefs

Write down any beliefs you have about money that might be holding you back. These beliefs often stem from past experiences, family, or cultural influences. Consider statements like:

"I'll never have enough money."
"People like me don't become wealthy."
"Money is the root of all problems."

Take some time to reflect on where these beliefs came from.
Did you hear them growing up?
Have you experienced moments where these beliefs seemed true?

____

____

____

____

JOURNAL ENTRY

Date:

What are the top 3 limiting beliefs I hold about money?

How have these beliefs affected my financial decisions?

Did I inherit any of these from my family or community?

How have those shaped my relationship with money?

"Do not wait; the time will never be 'just right.' Start where you stand."
— Napoleon Hill

Challenge Your Limited Beliefs

Use the space below to challenge each limiting belief by writing down evidence that contradicts it.
I'll give you an example to get you started!

LIMITED BELIEF	THE EVIDENCE
I'll never have enough money.	*I had enough money when I paid my rent/mortgage last month!*

JOURNAL ENTRY

Date:

What evidence do I have that challenges these limiting beliefs?

How can I start adopting new beliefs that align with my financial goals?

"The key to success is to focus on goals, not obstacles."
- Anonymous

POSITIVE AFFIRMATIONS

Create new positive affirmations that will guide your financial decisions moving forward. I'll give you an example below!

I am capable of managing my money well and building wealth.

REWRITE YOUR MONEY STORY

REFLECT AND REWRITE

Before you start the next exercise, take some time to reflect.

Think about your past experiences with money.

What were your earliest memories of money, and how did they shape your current financial behaviors?

This could be memories from childhood, lessons from family, or personal financial mistakes or wins.

START NOW

THE REFLECTION

Date:

What is my CURRENT money story?

How has my financial past influenced my present relationship with money?

"It's not about having more time, it's about making the time you have count."
- Anonymous

REWRITE YOUR MONEY STORY

THE NEW STORY

Now that you've identified your old money story, it's time to rewrite it with the mindset you want to adopt. Focus on empowerment, growth, and abundance. For example:

Your *old story* might have mentioned how you've always struggled with money because you were never taught how to manage it.

In contrast, your ***new story*** may speak to how you are now learning to manage your money and take control of your financial future.

START NOW

THE REWRITING

Date:

What is my NEW, EMPOWERING money story?

How does this new story align with my financial goals and the future I want to create?

"Success is not final, failure is not fatal: it is the courage to continue that counts."
— Winston Churchill

TAKE ACTION!

Money TALK$ Money TALK$ Money TALK$
YOUR | FINANCIAL | FUTURE

It's time to **TAKE ACTION** towards your new money story! Use the space below to identify small, actionable steps you can take to start living out your new money story.
I'll start you out with a couple of examples!

Ex.
Educate myself on spending plans.

Ex.
Create a plan to increase my savings.

MONTHLY RECAP

MONTH OF

THIS MONTH'S ACHIEVEMENTS

WHAT DO YOU FEEL WORKED THIS MONTH?

WHAT DO YOU FEEL DIDN'T WORK THIS MONTH?

THINGS TO DO MORE OF

MONTHLY GRATITUDE

Money TALK$

FINANCIAL LITERACY + EDUCATION

SECTION THREE

MONTHLY PLANNER

MONTH & YEAR

SUN	MON	TUE	WED	THU	FRI	SAT

TO DO:

THIS MONTH'S GOALS

MONTHLY AFFIRMATIONS

POSITIVE AFFIRMATION

“I AM worthy of financial security and abundance.

DEFINING "FINANCIAL LITERACY"

"Financial literacy" is the foundation for making informed decisions about your money.

Understanding the basic principles of managing, saving, investing, and protecting your finances will empower you to create a financially secure future. In this lesson, you'll learn key financial concepts that will help you navigate your financial journey with confidence.

Money TALK$ FACT

According to the 2024 TIAA Institute-GFLEC Personal Finance Index, financial literacy levels in the USA are notably low across generations, with Generation Z scoring the lowest, correctly answering only 37% of the surveyed questions.

In this section, you will be provided a thorough education of overall financial literacy including learning the terminology and key concepts. This knowledge helps you avoid debt, save for future goals, and prepare for emergencies.

Having financial literacy is important because it gives you control over your financial future. Without it, you might find yourself making poor financial decisions that could lead to serious, life-impacting debt or significant financial stress. For instance, understanding the importance of saving money can help you build a safety net for unexpected expenses, like medical bills or car repairs. It also empowers you to make informed choices about loans, credit cards, and investments, ensuring you get the best deals and avoid financial pitfalls.

FINANCIAL GLOSSARY

COMMON FINANCIAL TERMS TO KNOW

ASSETS

Resources with economic value that you own, such as property, stocks, or cash.

LIABILITIES

Debts or obligations you owe to others, such as loans, mortgages, or credit card balances.

NET WORTH

The total value of your assets minus your liabilities; a measure of financial health.

INCOME

Money you receive, typically from work, investments, or other sources.

EXPENSE

Money spent on goods, services, or obligations (e.g., rent, utilities, groceries).

LIQUIDITY

The ease with which an asset can be converted into cash without losing value.

DIVERSIFICATION

The practice of spreading investments across different assets to reduce risk.

RISK

The potential for losing money in an investment or financial transaction.

RETURN ON INVESTMENT (ROI)

The gain or loss generated by an investment, expressed as a percentage of the initial investment.

EQUITY: *The value of ownership in an asset, such as the portion of a home you own outright, minus any outstanding loans.*

FINANCIAL GLOSSARY

COMMON FINANCIAL TERMS TO KNOW

FIXED EXPENSES

Regular, predictable expenses, such as rent or car payments, that stay the same each month.

VARIABLE EXPENSES

Costs that change month to month, such as groceries or entertainment.

PRINCIPAL

The original sum of money borrowed or invested, excluding interest.

DIVIDENDS

Payments made by a company to its shareholders, usually from profits.

AMORTIZATION

The process of gradually paying off debt through scheduled payments of principal and interest.

ANNUAL PERCENTAGE RATE (APR)

The total cost of borrowing money, including interest & fees, expressed as a yearly percentage.

FICO SCORE

A type of credit score used by lenders to assess credit risk.

DEBT-TO-INCOME RATIO (DTI)

A ratio comparing your total monthly debt payments to your gross monthly income.

CASH FLOW

The net amount of cash being transferred in and out of your accounts (income vs. expenses).

CAPITAL GAINS: *The profit from selling an asset for more than its purchase price.*

KEY CONCEPTS OF FINANCIAL LITERACY

1

SPENDING PLANS

Spending plans create a plan for your money, allowing you to track how much you earn, spend, and save. A well-structured spending plan helps you manage your expenses, avoid debt, and work toward financial goals.

2

SAVING

Saving involves setting aside money for future needs or emergencies. A savings account helps you build financial security and achieve short- and long-term goals, such as buying a house, funding education, or retirement.

3

DEBT MANAGEMENT

Debt management is the process of handling and paying down debts responsibly. Whether it's credit card debt, student loans, or mortgages, understanding how to prioritize and pay off debt can save you money and reduce financial stress.

4

CREDIT SCORES

Your credit score is a numerical representation of your creditworthiness. It affects your ability to borrow money, secure loans, and obtain favorable interest rates. Higher credit scores lead to better financial opportunities.

5

INTEREST RATES

An interest rate is the percentage charged by lenders for borrowing money. It's also the percentage earned on savings and investments. Understanding how interest rates work helps you make better decisions about loans and savings.

KEY CONCEPTS OF FINANCIAL LITERACY

6 INVESTING

Investing is the act of allocating money into assets (e.g., stocks, bonds, real estate) with the goal of generating a return over time. Investing allows your money to grow, but it also carries risk.

7 EMERGENCY FUND

An emergency fund is money set aside for unexpected expenses, such as medical bills, car repairs, or job loss. Experts recommend saving three to six months' worth of living expenses in an emergency fund.

8 RETIREMENT ACCOUNTS

Retirement accounts, such as 401(k)s or IRAs, allow you to save and invest for the future while receiving tax advantages. The earlier you start saving for retirement, the more you benefit from compound interest.

9 COMPOUND INTEREST

Compound interest is the interest you earn on both your initial investment and the accumulated interest from previous periods. It helps your money grow faster over time, especially when you reinvest your earnings.

10 INFLATION

Inflation refers to the general increase in prices and the decrease in purchasing power of money over time. Understanding inflation helps you plan for long-term financial goals, as it impacts the value of your savings and investments.

LET'S TEST YOUR FINANCIAL LITERACY

Test your knowledge by answering the following questions. Write your answers down, and check the answer key at the end to see how well you did!

(1) What is a spending plan?

(2) What's the recommended amount of money to keep in an emergency fund?

(3) What does a high credit score help you with?

(4) What is compound interest?

(5) What is the main difference between fixed and variable expenses?

QUIZ LET'S TEST YOUR FINANCIAL LITERACY

(6) What does "ROI" stand for?

(7) What is inflation, and how does it impact your purchasing power?

(8) How does diversification reduce investment risk?

(9) What is the debt-to-income (DTI) ratio used for?

(10) What's the main purpose of an investment account?

(11) What does liquidity refer to in financial terms?

QUIZ LET'S TEST YOUR FINANCIAL LITERACY

(12) What are dividends, and who receives them?

(13) How do interest rates affect borrowing and saving?

(14) What is the difference between an asset and a liability?

(15) What is the benefit of starting to save for retirement early?

(16) What's the role of an amortization schedule?

(17) What is net worth, and how is it calculated?

QUIZ LET'S TEST YOUR FINANCIAL LITERACY

(18) What does "APR" stand for, and why is it important?

(19) How does inflation impact long-term savings?

(20) What are capital gains?

SEE ANSWER KEY

QUIZ LET'S TEST YOUR FINANCIAL LITERACY

FINANCIAL LITERACY QUIZ ANSWER KEY

1. A plan for how to allocate income to cover expenses, savings, and debt.

2. Three to six months' worth of living expenses.

3. Helps secure loans, lower interest rates, and better financial opportunities.

4. Interest earned on both the original investment and the accumulated interest.

5. Fixed expenses remain the same each month; variable expenses fluctuate.

6. Return on Investment.

7. Inflation is the rise in prices over time, reducing purchasing power.

8. By spreading investments across different assets, reducing the impact of any single asset's performance.

9. Measures the percentage of your income spent on debt payments, used by lenders to assess your ability to repay loans.

10. To grow wealth over time through the appreciation of assets or earned returns.

11. How easily an asset can be converted into cash without loss in value.

12. Payments made by companies to shareholders, usually from profits.

LET'S TEST YOUR FINANCIAL LITERACY

FINANCIAL LITERACY QUIZ ANSWER KEY

13. Higher interest rates make borrowing more expensive and saving more rewarding.

14. An asset is something you own that has value; a liability is something you owe.

15. More time for compound interest to grow the savings.

16. A schedule that outlines how loan payments are applied to principal and interest over time.

17. Net worth is your total assets minus total liabilities.

18. Annual Percentage Rate; it's the total cost of borrowing money, including fees and interest.

19. Inflation reduces the future value of savings, as money loses purchasing power over time.

20. Profit from selling an asset at a higher price than its purchase cost.

RATE YOUR KNOWLEDGE

Using the scale below, rate how you feel you scored on this quiz!

JOURNAL ENTRY

Date:

What part of managing your finances do you feel the least confident about (e.g., spending plans, investing, credit)?

How can gaining knowledge in that area change the way you handle your money?

"Success is not final, failure is not fatal: it is the courage to continue that counts."
— Winston Churchill

MONTHLY RECAP

MONTH OF

THIS MONTH'S ACHIEVEMENTS

WHAT DO YOU FEEL WORKED THIS MONTH?

WHAT DO YOU FEEL DIDN'T WORK THIS MONTH?

THINGS TO DO MORE OF

MONTHLY GRATITUDE

Money TALK$

MONTHLY TRACKING + REVIEW

THE 50-30-20 RULE

SECTION FOUR

MONTHLY PLANNER

MONTH & YEAR

SUN	MON	TUE	WED	THU	FRI	SAT

TO DO:

THIS MONTH'S GOALS

MONTHLY AFFIRMATIONS

POSITIVE AFFIRMATION

I AM
focused on building lasting wealth and wellbeing.

Money TALKS

MONTHLY TRACKING + REVIEW

Tracking and reviewing your finances is essential for building confidence and control over your money. The 50-30-20 Rule serves as a flexible framework to guide your spending and saving habits. It complements your spending plan by offering a broader perspective on how your income should be allocated:

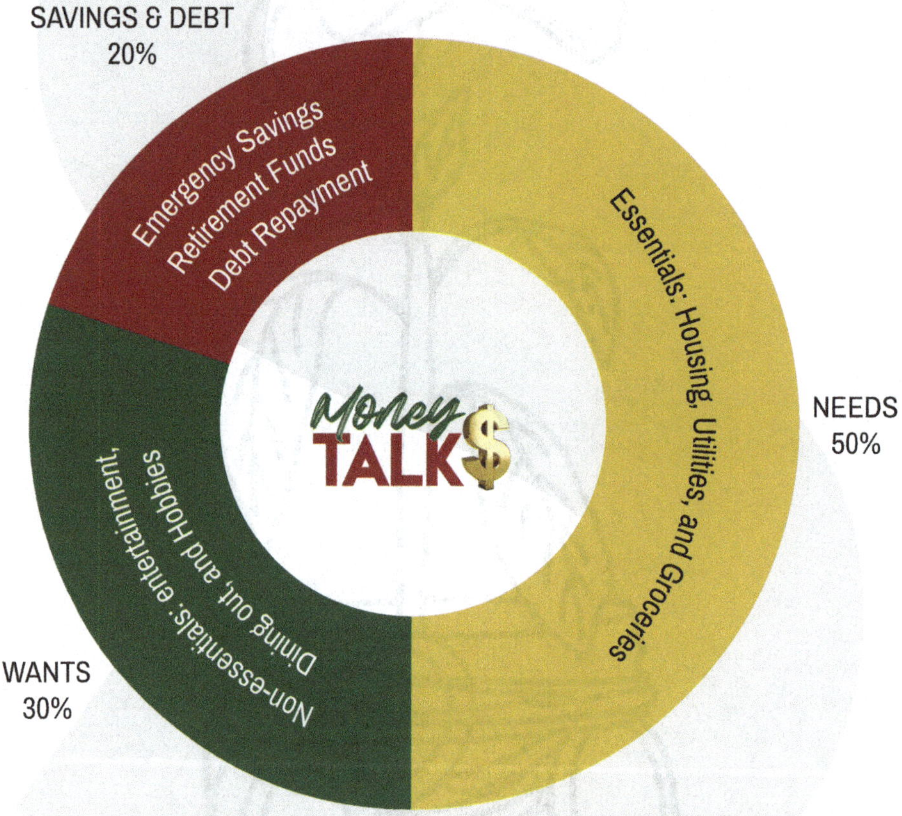

The 50-30-20 Rule simplifies financial decision-making by providing a balanced approach, ensuring you're covering your essentials, enjoying life responsibly, and saving for the future.

How the 50-30-20 Rule Complements Your Spending Plan

Your **spending plan** is where this framework becomes actionable. Think of the 50-30-20 Rule as the "blueprint" and your spending plan as the "execution." While the 50-30-20 Rule helps you allocate percentages to overarching categories, your spending plan breaks those categories into detailed, line-item expenses like rent, groceries, and savings deposits. Together, they provide both structure and flexibility to achieve financial stability.

- **Initial Creation:** Use the 50-30-20 framework as a starting point to create your spending plan.

- **Alignment Check:** Periodically review your plan to ensure your line-item spending reflects your 50-30-20 allocations.

Quarterly or As-Needed Recalibration

Consistency is key, but flexibility is necessary when life changes occur. That's why this planner includes **4 Quarterly or As-Needed 50-30-20 Trackers** to help you recalibrate your spending plan.

- **Quarterly Check-Ins:** Every three months, revisit your tracker to evaluate if your spending aligns with your goals and values. This regular reflection keeps you intentional without feeling overwhelmed.

- **Life-Triggered Revisions:** If you experience major changes—such as a shift in income, a new financial goal, or unexpected expenses—use an additional tracker to adapt your plan intentionally.

How to Use
The 50-30-20 Tracker

1. **Set Your Foundation:** Start with the tracker to create your first 50-30-20 allocation and ensure it reflects your financial reality.

2. **Maintain Consistency:** Use your spending plan monthly to track and execute your specific line items, keeping your allocations in mind.

3. **Quarterly Review:** Adjust your allocations quarterly to reflect any shifts in your financial situation, goals, or priorities.

4. **Adapt When Needed:** Use additional trackers during periods of significant life changes to ensure you stay on course.

Consistency Over Constant Change

The goal isn't to reallocate your percentages monthly but to use the 50-30-20 Rule as a guide for maintaining stability. With regular tracking, quarterly reviews, and as-needed recalibration, you'll stay empowered and intentional without unnecessary complexity.

This combination of the 50-30-20 Rule and a personalized spending plan gives you the flexibility to adapt while staying consistent, paving the way for financial wellbeing and lasting success.

50/30/20 TRACKER

MONTH + YEAR

MONTHLY BILLS - TRACK YOUR BILLS & PAYMENTS BELOW:

BILLS/EXPENSES	AMOUNT DUE	DUE ON	PAID ON	✓
Ex. Wells Fargo Home Mortgage	$1,850.00	02/01/2000	01/31/2000	☑
				☐
				☐
				☐
				☐
				☐
				☐
				☐
				☐
				☐
				☐
				☐
				☐
				☐
				☐
				☐
				☐
				☐
				☐
				☐
				☐
				☐
				☐
				☐
				☐
				☐
				☐
				☐
				☐
				☐
				☐

50/30/20 TRACKER

Based on your Monthly Bill Tracker, complete the 50/30/20 chart below to see how your actual spending compares to the percentages suggested for each category.

Total Monthly Income:	$		
Category & Suggested Percentages	Amount Allocated for this Category	Actual Amount Spent in this Category	Actual Percentage Spent in this Category
NEEDS (50%)	$	$	$
WANTS (30%)	$	$	$
SAVINGS (20%)	$	$	$

ASSESSMENT & ADJUSTMENTS

NEEDS

Did you overspend in this category this month?

○yes ○no

What adjustments will be made next month in this category?

Ex. Use coupons for groceries

Will these adjustments get you closer to your goal?

○yes ○no

WANTS

Did you overspend in this category this month?

○yes ○no

What adjustments will be made next month in this category?

Ex. Pack lunch from home.

Will these adjustments get you closer to your goal?

○yes ○no

SAVINGS

Did you have enough to save or make extra debt payments this month?

○yes ○no

What savings categories are you prioritizing with the leftover funds?

Ex. Capital One Payoff

Will focusing on these savings or repayment priorities get you closer to your goal?

○yes ○no

50/30/20 TRACKER

MONTH + YEAR

MONTHLY BILLS - TRACK YOUR BILLS & PAYMENTS BELOW:

BILLS/EXPENSES	AMOUNT DUE	DUE ON	PAID ON	✓
Ex. Wells Fargo Home Mortgage	*$1,850.00*	*02/01/2000*	*01/31/2000*	☑
				☐
				☐
				☐
				☐
				☐
				☐
				☐
				☐
				☐
				☐
				☐
				☐
				☐
				☐
				☐
				☐
				☐
				☐
				☐
				☐
				☐
				☐
				☐
				☐
				☐
				☐
				☐
				☐
				☐
				☐
				☐

50/30/20 TRACKER

Based on your Monthly Bill Tracker, complete the 50/30/20 chart below to see how your actual spending compares to the percentages suggested for each category.

Total Monthly Income:	$		
Category & Suggested Percentages	Amount Allocated for this Category	Actual Amount Spent in this Category	Actual Percentage Spent in this Category
NEEDS (50%)	$	$	$
WANTS (30%)	$	$	$
SAVINGS (20%)	$	$	$

ASSESSMENT & ADJUSTMENTS

NEEDS

Did you overspend in this category this month?

○yes ○no

What adjustments will be made next month in this category?

Ex. Use coupons for groceries

Will these adjustments get you closer to your goal?

○yes ○no

WANTS

Did you overspend in this category this month?

○yes ○no

What adjustments will be made next month in this category?

Ex. Pack lunch from home.

Will these adjustments get you closer to your goal?

○yes ○no

SAVINGS

Did you have enough to save or make extra debt payments this month?

○yes ○no

What savings categories are you prioritizing with the leftover funds?

Ex. Capital One Payoff

Will focusing on these savings or repayment priorities get you closer to your goal?

○yes ○no

50/30/20 TRACKER

MONTH + YEAR

MONTHLY BILLS - TRACK YOUR BILLS & PAYMENTS BELOW:

BILLS/EXPENSES	AMOUNT DUE	DUE ON	PAID ON	✓
Ex. Wells Fargo Home Mortgage	$1,850.00	02/01/2000	01/31/2000	☑
				☐
				☐
				☐
				☐
				☐
				☐
				☐
				☐
				☐
				☐
				☐
				☐
				☐
				☐
				☐
				☐
				☐
				☐
				☐
				☐
				☐
				☐
				☐
				☐
				☐
				☐
				☐
				☐
				☐
				☐
				☐

50/30/20 TRACKER

Based on your Monthly Bill Tracker, complete the 50/30/20 chart below to see how your actual spending compares to the percentages suggested for each category.

Total Monthly Income:	$		
Category & Suggested Percentages	Amount Allocated for this Category	Actual Amount Spent in this Category	Actual Percentage Spent in this Category
NEEDS (50%)	$	$	$
WANTS (30%)	$	$	$
SAVINGS (20%)	$	$	$

ASSESSMENT & ADJUSTMENTS

NEEDS

Did you overspend in this category this month?

O yes O no

What adjustments will be made next month in this category?

Ex. Use coupons for groceries

____

____

____

____

____

Will these adjustments get you closer to your goal?

O yes O no

WANTS

Did you overspend in this category this month?

O yes O no

What adjustments will be made next month in this category?

Ex. Pack lunch from home.

____

____

____

____

____

Will these adjustments get you closer to your goal?

O yes O no

SAVINGS

Did you have enough to save or make extra debt payments this month?

O yes O no

What savings categories are you prioritizing with the leftover funds?

Ex. Capital One Payoff

____

____

____

____

Will focusing on these savings or repayment priorities get you closer to your goal?

O yes O no

50/30/20 TRACKER

MONTH + YEAR

MONTHLY BILLS - TRACK YOUR BILLS & PAYMENTS BELOW:

BILLS/EXPENSES	AMOUNT DUE	DUE ON	PAID ON	✓
Ex. Wells Fargo Home Mortgage	$1,850.00	02/01/2000	01/31/2000	☑
				☐
				☐
				☐
				☐
				☐
				☐
				☐
				☐
				☐
				☐
				☐
				☐
				☐
				☐
				☐
				☐
				☐
				☐
				☐
				☐
				☐
				☐
				☐
				☐
				☐
				☐
				☐
				☐
				☐
				☐
				☐

50/30/20 TRACKER

Based on your Monthly Bill Tracker, complete the 50/30/20 chart below to see how your actual spending compares to the percentages suggested for each category.

Total Monthly Income:	$		
Category & Suggested Percentages	Amount Allocated for this Category	Actual Amount Spent in this Category	Actual Percentage Spent in this Category
NEEDS (50%)	$	$	$
WANTS (30%)	$	$	$
SAVINGS (20%)	$	$	$

ASSESSMENT & ADJUSTMENTS

NEEDS

Did you overspend in this category this month?

○yes ○no

What adjustments will be made next month in this category?

Ex. Use coupons for groceries

Will these adjustments get you closer to your goal?

○yes ○no

WANTS

Did you overspend in this category this month?

○yes ○no

What adjustments will be made next month in this category?

Ex. Pack lunch from home.

Will these adjustments get you closer to your goal?

○yes ○no

SAVINGS

Did you have enough to save or make extra debt payments this month?

○yes ○no

What savings categories are you prioritizing with the leftover funds?

Ex. Capital One Payoff

Will focusing on these savings or repayment priorities get you closer to your goal?

○yes ○no

JOURNAL ENTRY

Date:

What worked well this month? (e.g., I met my savings goal, kept my spending on entertainment low)

What are some areas for improvement next month? (e.g., I overspent on dining out, need to cut back on groceries)

"The best way to predict the future is to create it."
— Peter Drucker

MONTHLY RECAP

MONTH OF

THIS MONTH'S ACHIEVEMENTS

WHAT DO YOU FEEL WORKED THIS MONTH?

WHAT DO YOU FEEL DIDN'T WORK THIS MONTH?

THINGS TO DO MORE OF

MONTHLY GRATITUDE

Money TALK$

SPENDING PLAN

SECTION FIVE

MONTHLY PLANNER

MONTH & YEAR

SUN	MON	TUE	WED	THU	FRI	SAT

TO DO:

THIS MONTH'S GOALS

MONTHLY AFFIRMATIONS

POSITIVE AFFIRMATION

I OVERCOME challenges with resilience and confidence.

Money TALK$

Translating Goals into Action with Monthly Spending Plans

Your monthly spending plan is where vision meets action. While the **50-30-20 framework** provides the big-picture structure for your financial life, your spending plan translates those percentages into **specific, actionable line items** that reflect your goals, values, and day-to-day needs. This is your personalized roadmap for managing your money with intention and clarity.

Money TALK$ FACT

A 2024 study from the U.S. Bank reveals that only 41% of Americans reported they stick to a spending plan, highlighting a significant gap in financial management practices.

Source: www.usbank.com

A spending plan isn't just about controlling your money—it's about **putting you in control.** By organizing your income into detailed categories, you can:

- Ensure essential expenses are covered.
- Make space for what matters most to you.
- Proactively tackle debt and build meaningful savings.

Why Monthly Spending Plans Are Essential

Your spending plan is the foundation for financial stability, empowering you to:

1. **Spot Opportunities for Adjustment:** Track where your money is going and identify areas where you may be overspending or underspending.

2. **Prevent Financial Stress:** Having a plan reduces anxiety by ensuring you're prepared for unexpected expenses and can handle the "what-ifs" with confidence.

3. **Achieve Financial Milestones:** From saving for an emergency fund or a vacation to reaching long-term goals like homeownership or retirement, your spending plan keeps you moving forward.

A Tool for Confidence and Flexibility

A monthly spending plan isn't restrictive—it's **empowering.** It's a dynamic tool that evolves with your priorities and life circumstances. By regularly aligning your spending with your 50-30-20 framework, you'll have the clarity and confidence to stay in control, adjust when needed, and make progress toward the life you want.

With this planner, you'll have the templates and guidance to create and review your spending plan each month. This practice, paired with the 50-30-20 rule, equips you to:

- Balance immediate needs with future goals.
- Navigate financial challenges with ease.
- Stay focused on what truly matters.

Your spending plan isn't just a financial tool—it's your key to living with purpose, freedom, and financial peace of mind.

MONTHLY SPENDING GUIDE

Follow this **step-by-step guide** to build your personalized monthly spending plan.

Step 1: Calculate Your Monthly Income

Start by calculating your total monthly income. This includes:

- Your take-home pay from a full-time or part-time job.
- Any side income from freelancing, investments, or other sources.

If your income fluctuates, use an average of the last few months to estimate your monthly earnings.

INCOME SOURCE	AMOUNT
	$
	$
	$
	$
	$
	$
TOTAL MONTHLY INCOME:	$

MONTHLY SPENDING GUIDE

Step 2: List Your Fixed Expenses

Fixed expenses are the recurring monthly bills that typically stay the same each month. These include:

- Rent or mortgage payments
- Utilities (electricity, water, internet)
- Insurance (health, car, home)
- Loan payments (student loans, car loans)

FIXED MONTHLY EXPENSE	AMOUNT
Rent/Mortgage	$
Utilities	$
Insurances	$
Loan Payments	$
	$
	$
	$
	$

MONTHLY SPENDING GUIDE

FIXED MONTHLY EXPENSE	AMOUNT
	$
	$
	$
	$
	$
	$
	$
	$
	$
	$
	$
TOTAL FIXED EXPENSES:	$

Step 3: Estimate Your Variable Expenses

Variable expenses fluctuate from month-to-month.
These might include:

- Groceries
- Transportation (gas, ride-shares)
- Entertainment (movies, dining out)
- Personal care (clothing, grooming)

It's important to keep an eye on variable expenses since they can be adjusted to accommodate savings or debt repayment goals.

MONTHLY VARIABLES	AMOUNT
Groceries	$
Transportation/Travel	$
Entertainment	$
Personal Care	$
	$
	$
	$
	$

MONTHLY SPENDING GUIDE

MONTHLY VARIABLES	AMOUNT
	$
	$
	$
	$
	$
	$
	$
	$
	$
	$
	$
TOTAL VARIABLE EXPENSES:	$

Step 4: Set Your Savings Goals

A successful spending plan includes a clear plan for savings. Whether you're building an emergency fund, saving for a vacation, or investing for the future, it's essential to dedicate part of your income toward savings each month. Prioritize your savings goals, and consider automating savings transfers.

List your monthly savings goals and target amounts below:

SAVINGS/FUND	MONTHLY SAVING	TARGET AMOUNT
Emergency Fund	$	$
Retirement Fund	$	$
Vacation Fund	$	$
	$	$
	$	$
	$	$
	$	$
TOTAL GOALS:	$ /MO	$

Step 5: Review and Adjust

Now that you have a complete picture of your monthly income and expenses, review your spending plan. Make sure that your income covers all expenses and leaves room for savings. If you find yourself short, look for areas in your variable expenses where you can cut back.

Remember, a spending plan is flexible and should be adjusted as your financial situation changes.

Use the formula below to get a snapshot of your monthly spending plan:

Total Monthly Income $ ______ minus - **Total Monthly Expenses** $ ______

Remaining Monthly Money

= $ ______

If you have money left over, consider increasing your savings or debt payments.

If you're short, identify areas where you can reduce spending.

MONTHLY SPENDING GUIDE

Step 6: Track Your Spending

Tracking monthly spending is essential for managing your finances effectively. It allows you to see exactly where your money is going, which can help you identify spending patterns and areas where you might be able to cut back. By keeping a close eye on your expenditures, you can ensure that you are living within your means and avoiding unnecessary debt. This practice also helps you save money for future goals, such as vacations, buying a home, or building an emergency fund.

To help you with this, we are providing a Spending Plan Tracker that consists of 12 monthly sheets designed to help you track your income and expenses each month. By using these sheets, you can monitor your progress and see where adjustments may be needed. Whether it's cutting back on dining out or finding ways to save on utilities, these sheets will help you stay on top of your finances and achieve your financial goals. Use them consistently to build good financial habits and ensure a more secure financial future.

Throughout the month, use the Spending Plan Tracker to track your actual spending against your spending plan. Adjust your plan as needed to stay within your limits.

START YOUR SPENDING PLAN

MoneyTALK$ SPENDING PLAN TRACKER

____
MONTH + YEAR

Category		Projected	Actual	Difference
INCOME	EMPLOYMENT	$	$	$
	ADDT'L WORK	$	$	$
	OTHER INCOME	$	$	$
	TOTAL INCOME	$	$	$
FIXED EXPENSES	RENT/MORTGAGE	$	$	$
	INSURANCES	$	$	$
	LOAN PAYMENTS	$	$	$
	OTHER EXPENSES	$	$	$
	TOTAL FIXED EXP.	$	$	$
VARIABLE EXPENSES	GROCERIES	$	$	$
	TRANSPORTATION	$	$	$
	ENTERTAINMENT	$	$	$
	PERSONAL CARE	$	$	$
	OTHER VARIABLES	$	$	$
	TOTAL VARIABLES	$	$	$

CONTINUE ON NEXT PAGE →

Money TALK$ SPENDING PLAN TRACKER

Category		Projected	Actual	Difference
SAVINGS GOALS	EMERGENCY FUND	$	$	$
	RETIREMENT ACCT	$	$	$
	VACATION FUND	$	$	$
	OTHER SAVINGS	$	$	$
	TOTAL SAVINGS	$	$	$

ACTUAL SNAPSHOT & RECAP

Use the chart below to see an overall snapshot of your month.

Total Income refers to your actual total from the Income category of your spending plan tracker.

Total Expenses is the sum of all actual totals in the Fixed Expenses, Variable Expenses and Savings Goals categories from your spending plan tracker.

Month's Total Income

$

minus

\-

Month's Total Expenses

$

Money Leftover This Month

= **$**

QUICK TIPS FOR STAYING ON TRACK

- **Automate Savings:** Set up automatic transfers to your savings account each month to ensure you stay on track.
- **Monitor Your Spending:** Regularly check your actual spending compared to your planned spending plan to see where you might be overspending.
- **Adjust as Needed:** Life happens! If you find you need to adjust your spending plan during the month, that's okay. The goal is to stay flexible while working toward your financial goals.

Money TALK$ SPENDING PLAN TRACKER

MONTH + YEAR

Category		Projected	Actual	Difference
INCOME	EMPLOYMENT	$	$	$
	ADDT'L WORK	$	$	$
	OTHER INCOME	$	$	$
	TOTAL INCOME	$	$	$
FIXED EXPENSES	RENT/MORTGAGE	$	$	$
	INSURANCES	$	$	$
	LOAN PAYMENTS	$	$	$
	OTHER EXPENSES	$	$	$
	TOTAL FIXED EXP.	$	$	$
VARIABLE EXPENSES	GROCERIES	$	$	$
	TRANSPORTATION	$	$	$
	ENTERTAINMENT	$	$	$
	PERSONAL CARE	$	$	$
	OTHER VARIABLES	$	$	$
	TOTAL VARIABLES	$	$	$

CONTINUE ON NEXT PAGE →

Category		Projected	Actual	Difference
SAVINGS GOALS	EMERGENCY FUND	$	$	$
	RETIREMENT ACCT	$	$	$
	VACATION FUND	$	$	$
	OTHER SAVINGS	$	$	$
	TOTAL SAVINGS	$	$	$

ACTUAL SNAPSHOT & RECAP

Use the chart below to see an overall snapshot of your month.
Total Income refers to your actual total from the Income category of your spending plan tracker.

Total Expenses is the sum of all actual totals in the Fixed Expenses, Variable Expenses and Savings Goals categories from your spending plan tracker.

Month's Total Income		Month's Total Expenses
$	minus -	$

Money Leftover This Month

= $

QUICK TIPS FOR STAYING ON TRACK

- **Automate Savings:** Set up automatic transfers to your savings account each month to ensure you stay on track.
- **Monitor Your Spending:** Regularly check your actual spending compared to your planned spending plan to see where you might be overspending.
- **Adjust as Needed:** Life happens! If you find you need to adjust your spending plan during the month, that's okay. The goal is to stay flexible while working toward your financial goals.

Money TALK$ SPENDING PLAN TRACKER

____
MONTH + YEAR

Category		Projected	Actual	Difference
INCOME	EMPLOYMENT	$	$	$
	ADDT'L WORK	$	$	$
	OTHER INCOME	$	$	$
	TOTAL INCOME	$	$	$
FIXED EXPENSES	RENT/MORTGAGE	$	$	$
	INSURANCES	$	$	$
	LOAN PAYMENTS	$	$	$
	OTHER EXPENSES	$	$	$
	TOTAL FIXED EXP.	$	$	$
VARIABLE EXPENSES	GROCERIES	$	$	$
	TRANSPORTATION	$	$	$
	ENTERTAINMENT	$	$	$
	PERSONAL CARE	$	$	$
	OTHER VARIABLES	$	$	$
	TOTAL VARIABLES	$	$	$

CONTINUE ON NEXT PAGE ➡

Category		Projected	Actual	Difference
SAVINGS GOALS	EMERGENCY FUND	$	$	$
	RETIREMENT ACCT	$	$	$
	VACATION FUND	$	$	$
	OTHER SAVINGS	$	$	$
	TOTAL SAVINGS	$	$	$

ACTUAL SNAPSHOT & RECAP

Use the chart below to see an overall snapshot of your month.
Total Income refers to your actual total from the Income category of your spending plan tracker.

Total Expenses is the sum of all actual totals in the Fixed Expenses, Variable Expenses and Savings Goals categories from your spending plan tracker.

Month's Total Income		Month's Total Expenses
$	minus -	$

Money Leftover This Month

= $

QUICK TIPS FOR STAYING ON TRACK

- **Automate Savings:** Set up automatic transfers to your savings account each month to ensure you stay on track.
- **Monitor Your Spending:** Regularly check your actual spending compared to your planned spending plan to see where you might be overspending.
- **Adjust as Needed:** Life happens! If you find you need to adjust your spending plan during the month, that's okay. The goal is to stay flexible while working toward your financial goals.

Money TALK$ SPENDING PLAN TRACKER

MONTH + YEAR

Category		Projected	Actual	Difference
INCOME	EMPLOYMENT	$	$	$
	ADDT'L WORK	$	$	$
	OTHER INCOME	$	$	$
	TOTAL INCOME	$	$	$
FIXED EXPENSES	RENT/MORTGAGE	$	$	$
	INSURANCES	$	$	$
	LOAN PAYMENTS	$	$	$
	OTHER EXPENSES	$	$	$
	TOTAL FIXED EXP.	$	$	$
VARIABLE EXPENSES	GROCERIES	$	$	$
	TRANSPORTATION	$	$	$
	ENTERTAINMENT	$	$	$
	PERSONAL CARE	$	$	$
	OTHER VARIABLES	$	$	$
	TOTAL VARIABLES	$	$	$

CONTINUE ON NEXT PAGE ➡

Category		Projected	Actual	Difference
SAVINGS GOALS	EMERGENCY FUND	$	$	$
	RETIREMENT ACCT	$	$	$
	VACATION FUND	$	$	$
	OTHER SAVINGS	$	$	$
	TOTAL SAVINGS	$	$	$

ACTUAL SNAPSHOT & RECAP

Use the chart below to see an overall snapshot of your month.
Total Income refers to your actual total from the Income category of your spending plan tracker.

Total Expenses is the sum of all actual totals in the Fixed Expenses, Variable Expenses and Savings Goals categories from your spending plan tracker.

Month's Total Income		Month's Total Expenses
$	minus -	$

Money Leftover This Month

= $

QUICK TIPS FOR STAYING ON TRACK

- **Automate Savings:** Set up automatic transfers to your savings account each month to ensure you stay on track.
- **Monitor Your Spending:** Regularly check your actual spending compared to your planned spending plan to see where you might be overspending.
- **Adjust as Needed:** Life happens! If you find you need to adjust your spending plan during the month, that's okay. The goal is to stay flexible while working toward your financial goals.

Money TALK$ SPENDING PLAN TRACKER

MONTH + YEAR

Category		Projected	Actual	Difference
INCOME	EMPLOYMENT	$	$	$
	ADDT'L WORK	$	$	$
	OTHER INCOME	$	$	$
	TOTAL INCOME	$	$	$
FIXED EXPENSES	RENT/MORTGAGE	$	$	$
	INSURANCES	$	$	$
	LOAN PAYMENTS	$	$	$
	OTHER EXPENSES	$	$	$
	TOTAL FIXED EXP.	$	$	$
VARIABLE EXPENSES	GROCERIES	$	$	$
	TRANSPORTATION	$	$	$
	ENTERTAINMENT	$	$	$
	PERSONAL CARE	$	$	$
	OTHER VARIABLES	$	$	$
	TOTAL VARIABLES	$	$	$

CONTINUE ON NEXT PAGE

Category		Projected	Actual	Difference
SAVINGS GOALS	EMERGENCY FUND	$	$	$
	RETIREMENT ACCT	$	$	$
	VACATION FUND	$	$	$
	OTHER SAVINGS	$	$	$
	TOTAL SAVINGS	$	$	$

ACTUAL SNAPSHOT & RECAP

Use the chart below to see an overall snapshot of your month.
Total Income refers to your actual total from the Income category of your spending plan tracker.

Total Expenses is the sum of all actual totals in the Fixed Expenses, Variable Expenses and Savings Goals categories from your spending plan tracker.

Month's Total Income $ ______ minus - **Month's Total Expenses** $ ______

Money Leftover This Month
= $ ______

QUICK TIPS FOR STAYING ON TRACK

- **Automate Savings:** Set up automatic transfers to your savings account each month to ensure you stay on track.
- **Monitor Your Spending:** Regularly check your actual spending compared to your planned spending plan to see where you might be overspending.
- **Adjust as Needed:** Life happens! If you find you need to adjust your spending plan during the month, that's okay. The goal is to stay flexible while working toward your financial goals.

Money TALK$ SPENDING PLAN TRACKER

MONTH + YEAR

Category		Projected	Actual	Difference
INCOME	EMPLOYMENT	$	$	$
	ADDT'L WORK	$	$	$
	OTHER INCOME	$	$	$
	TOTAL INCOME	$	$	$
FIXED EXPENSES	RENT/MORTGAGE	$	$	$
	INSURANCES	$	$	$
	LOAN PAYMENTS	$	$	$
	OTHER EXPENSES	$	$	$
	TOTAL FIXED EXP.	$	$	$
VARIABLE EXPENSES	GROCERIES	$	$	$
	TRANSPORTATION	$	$	$
	ENTERTAINMENT	$	$	$
	PERSONAL CARE	$	$	$
	OTHER VARIABLES	$	$	$
	TOTAL VARIABLES	$	$	$

CONTINUE ON NEXT PAGE

Category		Projected	Actual	Difference
SAVINGS GOALS	EMERGENCY FUND	$	$	$
	RETIREMENT ACCT	$	$	$
	VACATION FUND	$	$	$
	OTHER SAVINGS	$	$	$
	TOTAL SAVINGS	$	$	$

ACTUAL SNAPSHOT & RECAP

Use the chart below to see an overall snapshot of your month.
Total Income refers to your actual total from the Income category of your spending plan tracker.

Total Expenses is the sum of all actual totals in the Fixed Expenses, Variable Expenses and Savings Goals categories from your spending plan tracker.

Month's Total Income		Month's Total Expenses
$	minus -	$

Money Leftover This Month

= $

QUICK TIPS FOR STAYING ON TRACK

- **Automate Savings:** Set up automatic transfers to your savings account each month to ensure you stay on track.
- **Monitor Your Spending:** Regularly check your actual spending compared to your planned spending plan to see where you might be overspending.
- **Adjust as Needed:** Life happens! If you find you need to adjust your spending plan during the month, that's okay. The goal is to stay flexible while working toward your financial goals.

Money TALK$ SPENDING PLAN TRACKER

MONTH + YEAR

Category		Projected	Actual	Difference
INCOME	EMPLOYMENT	$	$	$
	ADDT'L WORK	$	$	$
	OTHER INCOME	$	$	$
	TOTAL INCOME	$	$	$
FIXED EXPENSES	RENT/MORTGAGE	$	$	$
	INSURANCES	$	$	$
	LOAN PAYMENTS	$	$	$
	OTHER EXPENSES	$	$	$
	TOTAL FIXED EXP.	$	$	$
VARIABLE EXPENSES	GROCERIES	$	$	$
	TRANSPORTATION	$	$	$
	ENTERTAINMENT	$	$	$
	PERSONAL CARE	$	$	$
	OTHER VARIABLES	$	$	$
	TOTAL VARIABLES	$	$	$

CONTINUE ON NEXT PAGE →

Money TALK$ SPENDING PLAN TRACKER

Category		Projected	Actual	Difference
SAVINGS GOALS	EMERGENCY FUND	$	$	$
	RETIREMENT ACCT	$	$	$
	VACATION FUND	$	$	$
	OTHER SAVINGS	$	$	$
	TOTAL SAVINGS	$	$	$

ACTUAL SNAPSHOT & RECAP

Use the chart below to see an overall snapshot of your month.

Total Income refers to your actual total from the Income category of your spending plan tracker.

Total Expenses is the sum of all actual totals in the Fixed Expenses, Variable Expenses and Savings Goals categories from your spending plan tracker.

Month's Total Income $ ______ minus - **Month's Total Expenses** $ ______

Money Leftover This Month

= $ ______

QUICK TIPS FOR STAYING ON TRACK

- **Automate Savings:** Set up automatic transfers to your savings account each month to ensure you stay on track.
- **Monitor Your Spending:** Regularly check your actual spending compared to your planned spending plan to see where you might be overspending.
- **Adjust as Needed:** Life happens! If you find you need to adjust your spending plan during the month, that's okay. The goal is to stay flexible while working toward your financial goals.

Money TALK$ SPENDING PLAN TRACKER

MONTH + YEAR

Category		Projected	Actual	Difference
INCOME	EMPLOYMENT	$	$	$
	ADDT'L WORK	$	$	$
	OTHER INCOME	$	$	$
	TOTAL INCOME	$	$	$
FIXED EXPENSES	RENT/MORTGAGE	$	$	$
	INSURANCES	$	$	$
	LOAN PAYMENTS	$	$	$
	OTHER EXPENSES	$	$	$
	TOTAL FIXED EXP.	$	$	$
VARIABLE EXPENSES	GROCERIES	$	$	$
	TRANSPORTATION	$	$	$
	ENTERTAINMENT	$	$	$
	PERSONAL CARE	$	$	$
	OTHER VARIABLES	$	$	$
	TOTAL VARIABLES	$	$	$

CONTINUE ON NEXT PAGE

Money TALK$ SPENDING PLAN TRACKER

Category		Projected	Actual	Difference
SAVINGS GOALS	EMERGENCY FUND	$	$	$
	RETIREMENT ACCT	$	$	$
	VACATION FUND	$	$	$
	OTHER SAVINGS	$	$	$
	TOTAL SAVINGS	$	$	$

ACTUAL SNAPSHOT & RECAP

Use the chart below to see an overall snapshot of your month.
Total Income refers to your actual total from the Income category of your spending plan tracker.

Total Expenses is the sum of all actual totals in the Fixed Expenses, Variable Expenses and Savings Goals categories from your spending plan tracker.

Month's Total Income		**Month's Total Expenses**
$	minus -	$

Money Leftover This Month

= $

QUICK TIPS FOR STAYING ON TRACK

- **Automate Savings:** Set up automatic transfers to your savings account each month to ensure you stay on track.
- **Monitor Your Spending:** Regularly check your actual spending compared to your planned spending plan to see where you might be overspending.
- **Adjust as Needed:** Life happens! If you find you need to adjust your spending plan during the month, that's okay. The goal is to stay flexible while working toward your financial goals.

Money TALK$ SPENDING PLAN TRACKER

MONTH + YEAR

Category		Projected	Actual	Difference
INCOME	EMPLOYMENT	$	$	$
	ADDT'L WORK	$	$	$
	OTHER INCOME	$	$	$
	TOTAL INCOME	$	$	$
FIXED EXPENSES	RENT/MORTGAGE	$	$	$
	INSURANCES	$	$	$
	LOAN PAYMENTS	$	$	$
	OTHER EXPENSES	$	$	$
	TOTAL FIXED EXP.	$	$	$
VARIABLE EXPENSES	GROCERIES	$	$	$
	TRANSPORTATION	$	$	$
	ENTERTAINMENT	$	$	$
	PERSONAL CARE	$	$	$
	OTHER VARIABLES	$	$	$
	TOTAL VARIABLES	$	$	$

CONTINUE ON NEXT PAGE →

Category		Projected	Actual	Difference
SAVINGS GOALS	EMERGENCY FUND	$	$	$
	RETIREMENT ACCT	$	$	$
	VACATION FUND	$	$	$
	OTHER SAVINGS	$	$	$
	TOTAL SAVINGS	$	$	$

ACTUAL SNAPSHOT & RECAP

Use the chart below to see an overall snapshot of your month.

Total Income refers to your actual total from the Income category of your spending plan tracker.

Total Expenses is the sum of all actual totals in the Fixed Expenses, Variable Expenses and Savings Goals categories from your spending plan tracker.

Month's Total Income $ ______ minus - **Month's Total Expenses** $ ______

Money Leftover This Month

= $ ______

QUICK TIPS FOR STAYING ON TRACK

- **Automate Savings:** Set up automatic transfers to your savings account each month to ensure you stay on track.
- **Monitor Your Spending:** Regularly check your actual spending compared to your planned spending plan to see where you might be overspending.
- **Adjust as Needed:** Life happens! If you find you need to adjust your spending plan during the month, that's okay. The goal is to stay flexible while working toward your financial goals.

Money TALK$ SPENDING PLAN TRACKER

MONTH + YEAR ____________________

Category		Projected	Actual	Difference
INCOME	EMPLOYMENT	$	$	$
	ADDT'L WORK	$	$	$
	OTHER INCOME	$	$	$
	TOTAL INCOME	$	$	$
FIXED EXPENSES	RENT/MORTGAGE	$	$	$
	INSURANCES	$	$	$
	LOAN PAYMENTS	$	$	$
	OTHER EXPENSES	$	$	$
	TOTAL FIXED EXP.	$	$	$
VARIABLE EXPENSES	GROCERIES	$	$	$
	TRANSPORTATION	$	$	$
	ENTERTAINMENT	$	$	$
	PERSONAL CARE	$	$	$
	OTHER VARIABLES	$	$	$
	TOTAL VARIABLES	$	$	$

CONTINUE ON NEXT PAGE →

Money TALK$ SPENDING PLAN TRACKER

Category		Projected	Actual	Difference
SAVINGS GOALS	EMERGENCY FUND	$	$	$
	RETIREMENT ACCT	$	$	$
	VACATION FUND	$	$	$
	OTHER SAVINGS	$	$	$
	TOTAL SAVINGS	$	$	$

ACTUAL SNAPSHOT & RECAP

Use the chart below to see an overall snapshot of your month.

Total Income refers to your actual total from the Income category of your spending plan tracker.

Total Expenses is the sum of all actual totals in the Fixed Expenses, Variable Expenses and Savings Goals categories from your spending plan tracker.

Month's Total Income $ minus - **Month's Total Expenses** $

Money Leftover This Month

= $

QUICK TIPS FOR STAYING ON TRACK

- **Automate Savings:** Set up automatic transfers to your savings account each month to ensure you stay on track.
- **Monitor Your Spending:** Regularly check your actual spending compared to your planned spending plan to see where you might be overspending.
- **Adjust as Needed:** Life happens! If you find you need to adjust your spending plan during the month, that's okay. The goal is to stay flexible while working toward your financial goals.

Money TALK$ SPENDING PLAN TRACKER

MONTH + YEAR

Category		Projected	Actual	Difference
INCOME	EMPLOYMENT	$	$	$
	ADDT'L WORK	$	$	$
	OTHER INCOME	$	$	$
	TOTAL INCOME	$	$	$
FIXED EXPENSES	RENT/MORTGAGE	$	$	$
	INSURANCES	$	$	$
	LOAN PAYMENTS	$	$	$
	OTHER EXPENSES	$	$	$
	TOTAL FIXED EXP.	$	$	$
VARIABLE EXPENSES	GROCERIES	$	$	$
	TRANSPORTATION	$	$	$
	ENTERTAINMENT	$	$	$
	PERSONAL CARE	$	$	$
	OTHER VARIABLES	$	$	$
	TOTAL VARIABLES	$	$	$

CONTINUE ON NEXT PAGE ➡

Category		Projected	Actual	Difference
SAVINGS GOALS	EMERGENCY FUND	$	$	$
	RETIREMENT ACCT	$	$	$
	VACATION FUND	$	$	$
	OTHER SAVINGS	$	$	$
	TOTAL SAVINGS	$	$	$

ACTUAL SNAPSHOT & RECAP

Use the chart below to see an overall snapshot of your month.
Total Income refers to your actual total from the Income category of your spending plan tracker.

Total Expenses is the sum of all actual totals in the Fixed Expenses, Variable Expenses and Savings Goals categories from your spending plan tracker.

Month's Total Income		Month's Total Expenses
$	minus -	$

Money Leftover This Month

= $

QUICK TIPS FOR STAYING ON TRACK

- **Automate Savings:** Set up automatic transfers to your savings account each month to ensure you stay on track.
- **Monitor Your Spending:** Regularly check your actual spending compared to your planned spending plan to see where you might be overspending.
- **Adjust as Needed:** Life happens! If you find you need to adjust your spending plan during the month, that's okay. The goal is to stay flexible while working toward your financial goals.

Money TALK$ SPENDING PLAN TRACKER

____
MONTH + YEAR

Category		Projected	Actual	Difference
INCOME	EMPLOYMENT	$	$	$
	ADDT'L WORK	$	$	$
	OTHER INCOME	$	$	$
	TOTAL INCOME	$	$	$
FIXED EXPENSES	RENT/MORTGAGE	$	$	$
	INSURANCES	$	$	$
	LOAN PAYMENTS	$	$	$
	OTHER EXPENSES	$	$	$
	TOTAL FIXED EXP.	$	$	$
VARIABLE EXPENSES	GROCERIES	$	$	$
	TRANSPORTATION	$	$	$
	ENTERTAINMENT	$	$	$
	PERSONAL CARE	$	$	$
	OTHER VARIABLES	$	$	$
	TOTAL VARIABLES	$	$	$

CONTINUE ON NEXT PAGE →

Money TALK$ SPENDING PLAN TRACKER

Category		Projected	Actual	Difference
SAVINGS GOALS	EMERGENCY FUND	$	$	$
	RETIREMENT ACCT	$	$	$
	VACATION FUND	$	$	$
	OTHER SAVINGS	$	$	$
	TOTAL SAVINGS	$	$	$

ACTUAL SNAPSHOT & RECAP

Use the chart below to see an overall snapshot of your month.
Total Income refers to your actual total from the Income category of your spending plan tracker.

Total Expenses is the sum of all actual totals in the Fixed Expenses, Variable Expenses and Savings Goals categories from your spending plan tracker.

Month's Total Income

$

minus
-

Month's Total Expenses

$

Money Leftover This Month

= $

QUICK TIPS FOR STAYING ON TRACK

- **Automate Savings:** Set up automatic transfers to your savings account each month to ensure you stay on track.
- **Monitor Your Spending:** Regularly check your actual spending compared to your planned spending plan to see where you might be overspending.
- **Adjust as Needed:** Life happens! If you find you need to adjust your spending plan during the month, that's okay. The goal is to stay flexible while working toward your financial goals.

MONTHLY RECAP

MONTH OF

THIS MONTH'S ACHIEVEMENTS

WHAT DO YOU FEEL WORKED THIS MONTH?

WHAT DO YOU FEEL DIDN'T WORK THIS MONTH?

THINGS TO DO MORE OF

MONTHLY GRATITUDE

Money TALK$

DEBT PAYOFF ACCELERATION + CREDIT UTILIZATION

SECTION SIX

MONTHLY PLANNER

MONTH & YEAR

SUN	MON	TUE	WED	THU	FRI	SAT

TO DO:

THIS MONTH'S GOALS

MONTHLY AFFIRMATIONS

POSITIVE AFFIRMATION

I MANAGE my finances with clarity and purpose.

DEBT PAYOFF ACCELERATION

Paying off debt requires a strategy. In this section, you'll explore three powerful methods for accelerating debt repayment: **Debt Snowball**, **Debt Avalanche**, and **Debt Consolidation**. Understanding these approaches will help you determine the best plan for your financial situation and make consistent progress toward becoming debt-free.

DEBT SNOWBALL

HOW IT WORKS Focuses on paying off the smallest debt first, regardless of interest rate. Once the smallest debt is paid off, roll that payment into the next smallest debt, creating momentum as you see your balances drop one by one.

WHO IT'S FOR Those who need quick wins and motivation by seeing small debts disappear first.

PROS	CONS
• Psychological boosts and motivation • Builds momentum early	• May cost more in interest over time if high interest debts are left for later

DEBT AVALANCHE

HOW IT WORKS Prioritize paying off the debt with the highest interest rate first. Once the highest-interest debt is paid off, roll that payment into the next highest interest rate debt. This method minimizes the total interest paid over time.

WHO IT'S FOR Those who want to minimize the amount of interest paid and can stay disciplined even when progress feels slow at first.

PROS	CONS
• Saves the most money in interest. • More cost-efficient overall	• Progress may feel slow especially if higher interest debt has a large balance

Which method may best fit your financial need?

- ○ **Debt Snowball:** I prefer quick wins and clearing small debts first for motivation.
- ○ **Debt Avalanche:** I want to save more money in interest and tackle high-interest debts first.

DEBT CONSOLIDATION

Debt Consolidation is another debt repayment option that combines multiple debts into a single loan or line of credit, typically at a lower interest rate. This can simplify your payments and potentially reduce the overall interest you pay, especially if your current debts have high interest rates. **Debt consolidation** is typically done through:

Personal Loan	*Balance Transfer Credit Card*	*Home Equity Loan or Line of Credit*
CONSOLIDATION LOAN	FOR CREDIT CARD DEBT	FOR SECURED DEBT

HOW DEBT CONSOLIDATION WORKS

(1) You take out a loan or use a balance transfer card to pay off multiple high-interest debts.

(2) Now, you only need to make one monthly payment to the new loan or credit card, instead of juggling several different payments.

(3) Ideally, the new loan has a lower interest rate, saving you money over time.

Pros of Debt Consolidation

Simplifies Your Payments
You only have one monthly payment instead of managing multiple debts.

Potential Lower Interest Rate
If you qualify for a lower interest rate, you can save on interest costs.

Boosts Credit Score
By reducing the number of outstanding debts, you may improve your credit score over time.

Cons of Debt Consolidation

May Not Solve Underlying Spending Habits
Consolidating your debt won't change your spending behavior. Without discipline, you may accumulate more debt.

Fees
Some debt consolidation loans and balance transfer cards come with fees, such as balance transfer fees or loan origination fees.

Collateral Risk
If you use a secured loan (like a home equity loan), your home is at risk if you fail to repay the loan.

DETERMINE IF DEBT CONSOLIDATION OPTION IS BEST FOR YOU. →

Debt Consolidation may be a good option for you if:

- [ ] You have high-interest debt and can secure a lower interest rate.
- [ ] You want to simplify your payments and focus on a single debt repayment plan.
- [ ] You are committed to avoiding new debt once your existing debts are consolidated.

Debt Consolidation may NOT be a good option for you if:

- [ ] You haven't addressed the spending habits that caused your debt.
- [ ] The fees associated with debt consolidation outweigh the potential savings in interest.
- [ ] You cannot secure a lower interest rate.

DEBT PRIORITIZATION

HOW TO EFFECTIVELY TACKLE DEBT

Once you understand the different debt repayment strategies, it's important to prioritize your debts based on urgency and long-term impact. Here's how to prioritize your debts:

Step 1: List All Your Debts

Utilize the Debt List to compile a complete list of all your debts, including:

- The type of debt (credit card, student loan, mortgage, etc.)
- The total balance owed
- The interest rate (APR)
- The minimum monthly payment

This will help you compare and decide which debts to prioritize.

Step 2: Choose Your Debt Payoff Strategy

Utilize the Debt Payoff Tracker to track monthly progress.

Debt Snowball: Pay off the smallest debt first. This method is great for staying motivated.

Debt Avalanche: Pay off the highest-interest debt first to save the most money on interest.

Debt Consolidation: If you have multiple high-interest debts, consider consolidating them into one lower-interest loan.

CONTINUE TO THE DEBT LIST

DEBT LIST

Use this page to compile a complete list of all your debts. Then, track your payoff method for each debt using the Debt Payoff Tracker!

CREDITOR/ DEBT NAME	TOTAL BALANCE	INTEREST RATE	MINIMUM MONTHLY PAYMENT
Wells Fargo Credit Card	$11,287.00	8.0%	$349.00

DEBT PAYOFF TRACKER

CREDITOR OR CONSOLIDATED LOAN

ACCOUNT #

ACCOUNT BALANCE

MONTHLY DUE DATE

INTEREST RATE

GOAL PAYOFF DATE

MINIMUM PAYMENT

DATE	PAYMENT MADE	BALANCE	NOTES

VISUAL PAYOFF PROGRESS

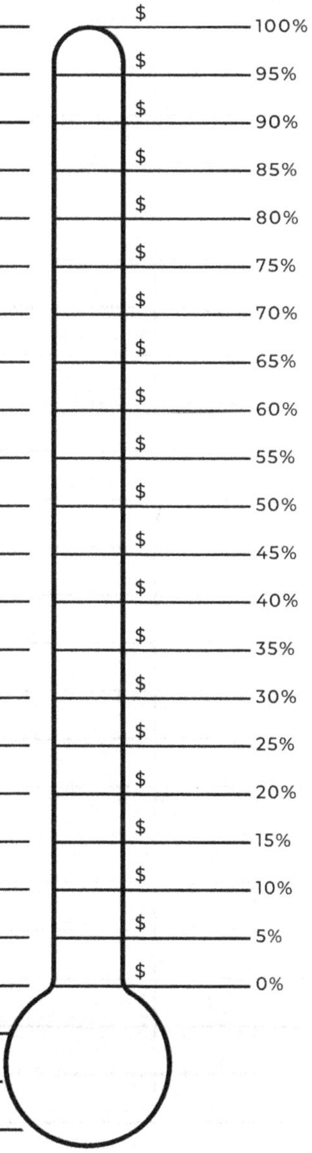

DEBT PAYOFF TRACKER

CREDITOR OR CONSOLIDATED LOAN

ACCOUNT #

ACCOUNT BALANCE

MONTHLY DUE DATE

INTEREST RATE

GOAL PAYOFF DATE

MINIMUM PAYMENT

DATE	PAYMENT MADE	BALANCE	NOTES

VISUAL PAYOFF PROGRESS

$ 100%
$ 95%
$ 90%
$ 85%
$ 80%
$ 75%
$ 70%
$ 65%
$ 60%
$ 55%
$ 50%
$ 45%
$ 40%
$ 35%
$ 30%
$ 25%
$ 20%
$ 15%
$ 10%
$ 5%
$ 0%

DEBT PAYOFF TRACKER

CREDITOR OR CONSOLIDATED LOAN

ACCOUNT #

ACCOUNT BALANCE

MONTHLY DUE DATE

INTEREST RATE

GOAL PAYOFF DATE

MINIMUM PAYMENT

DATE	PAYMENT MADE	BALANCE	NOTES

VISUAL PAYOFF PROGRESS

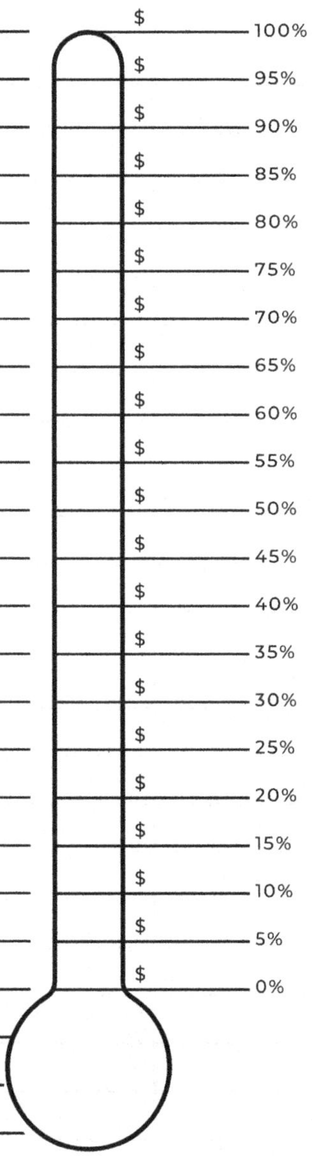

DEBT PAYOFF TRACKER

CREDITOR OR CONSOLIDATED LOAN	ACCOUNT #

ACCOUNT BALANCE	MONTHLY DUE DATE	INTEREST RATE

GOAL PAYOFF DATE	MINIMUM PAYMENT

DATE	PAYMENT MADE	BALANCE	NOTES

VISUAL PAYOFF PROGRESS

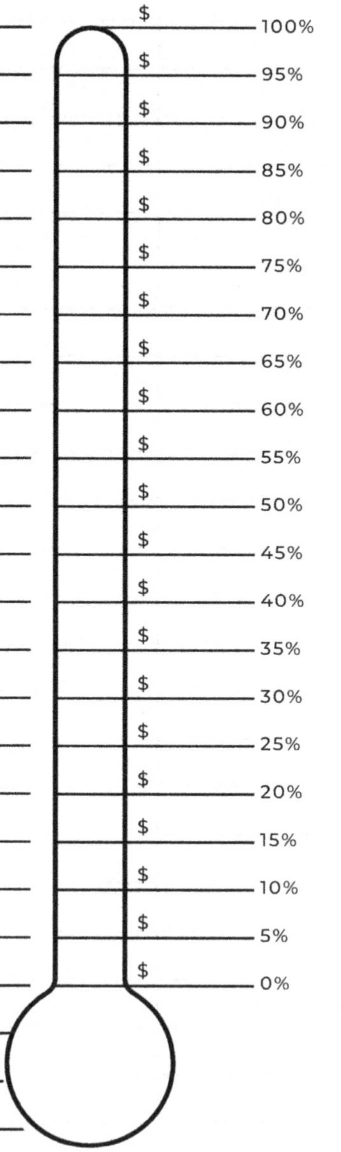

DEBT PAYOFF TRACKER

CREDITOR OR CONSOLIDATED LOAN

ACCOUNT #

ACCOUNT BALANCE

MONTHLY DUE DATE

INTEREST RATE

GOAL PAYOFF DATE

MINIMUM PAYMENT

DATE	PAYMENT MADE	BALANCE	NOTES

VISUAL PAYOFF PROGRESS

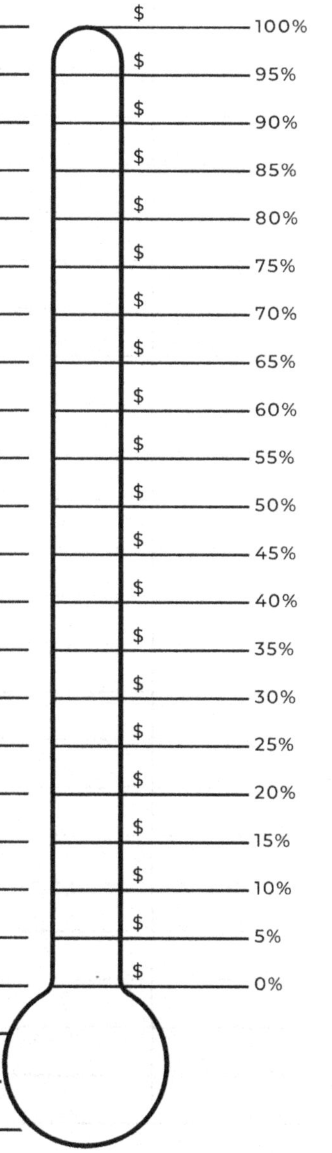

DEBT PAYOFF TRACKER

CREDITOR OR CONSOLIDATED LOAN	ACCOUNT #

ACCOUNT BALANCE	MONTHLY DUE DATE	INTEREST RATE

GOAL PAYOFF DATE	MINIMUM PAYMENT

DATE	PAYMENT MADE	BALANCE	NOTES

VISUAL PAYOFF PROGRESS

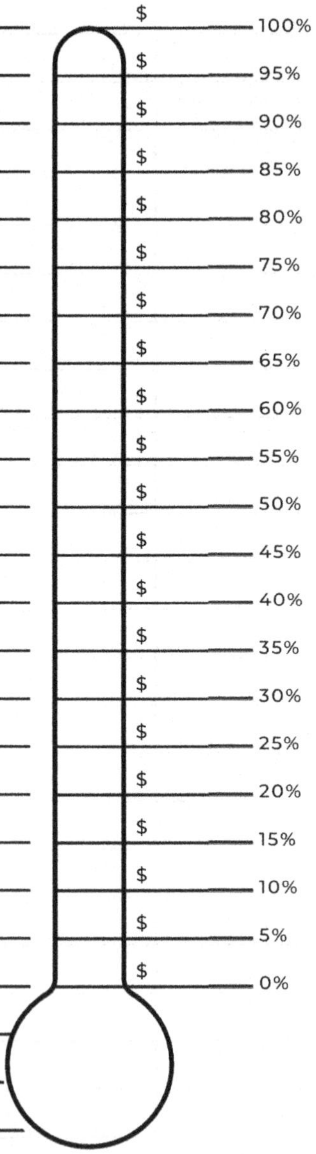

DEBT PAYOFF TRACKER

CREDITOR OR CONSOLIDATED LOAN

ACCOUNT #

ACCOUNT BALANCE

MONTHLY DUE DATE

INTEREST RATE

GOAL PAYOFF DATE

MINIMUM PAYMENT

DATE	PAYMENT MADE	BALANCE	NOTES

VISUAL PAYOFF PROGRESS

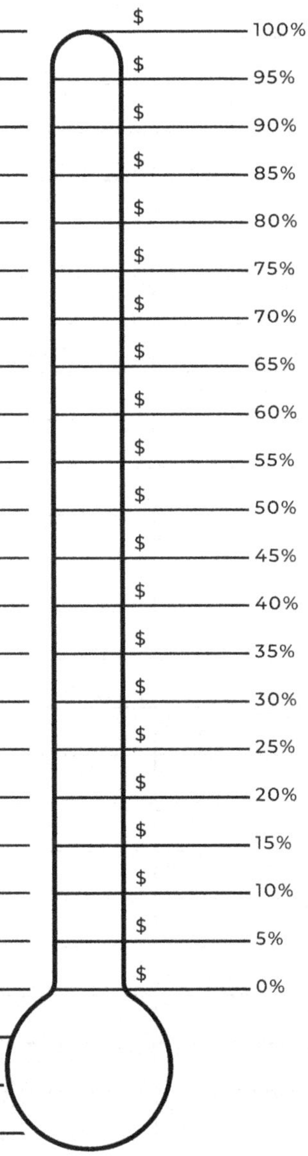

DEBT PAYOFF TRACKER

CREDITOR OR CONSOLIDATED LOAN

ACCOUNT #

ACCOUNT BALANCE

MONTHLY DUE DATE

INTEREST RATE

GOAL PAYOFF DATE

MINIMUM PAYMENT

DATE	PAYMENT MADE	BALANCE	NOTES

VISUAL PAYOFF PROGRESS

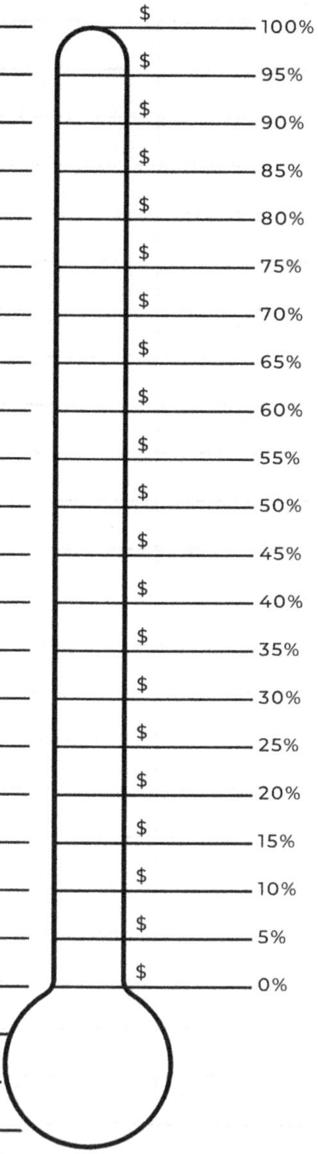

DEBT PAYOFF TRACKER

CREDITOR OR CONSOLIDATED LOAN

ACCOUNT #

ACCOUNT BALANCE

MONTHLY DUE DATE

INTEREST RATE

GOAL PAYOFF DATE

MINIMUM PAYMENT

VISUAL PAYOFF PROGRESS

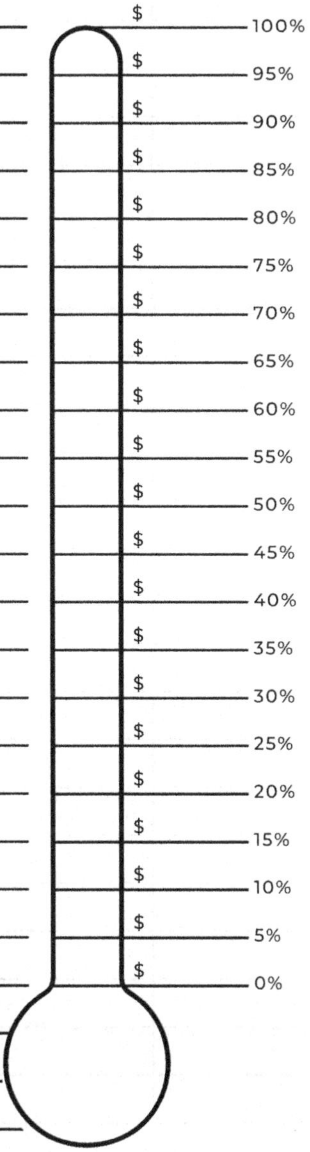

DATE	PAYMENT MADE	BALANCE	NOTES

DEBT PAYOFF TRACKER

CREDITOR OR CONSOLIDATED LOAN

ACCOUNT #

ACCOUNT BALANCE

MONTHLY DUE DATE

INTEREST RATE

GOAL PAYOFF DATE

MINIMUM PAYMENT

DATE	PAYMENT MADE	BALANCE	NOTES

VISUAL PAYOFF PROGRESS

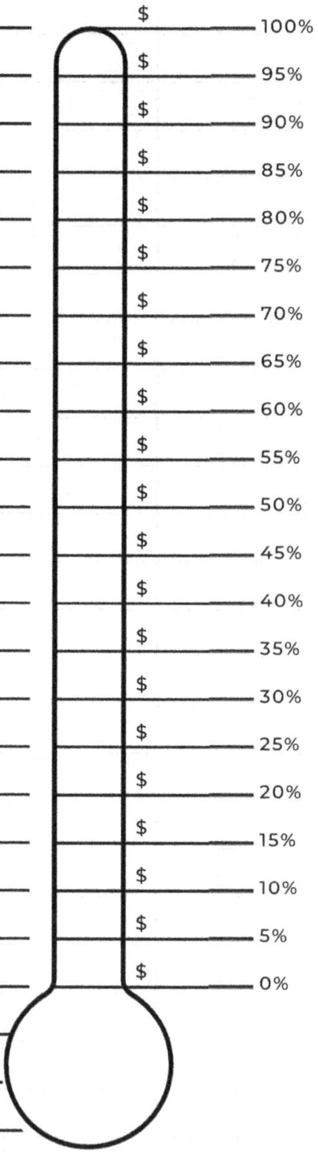

DEBT PAYOFF TRACKER

CREDITOR OR CONSOLIDATED LOAN

ACCOUNT #

ACCOUNT BALANCE

MONTHLY DUE DATE

INTEREST RATE

GOAL PAYOFF DATE

MINIMUM PAYMENT

DATE	PAYMENT MADE	BALANCE	NOTES

VISUAL PAYOFF PROGRESS

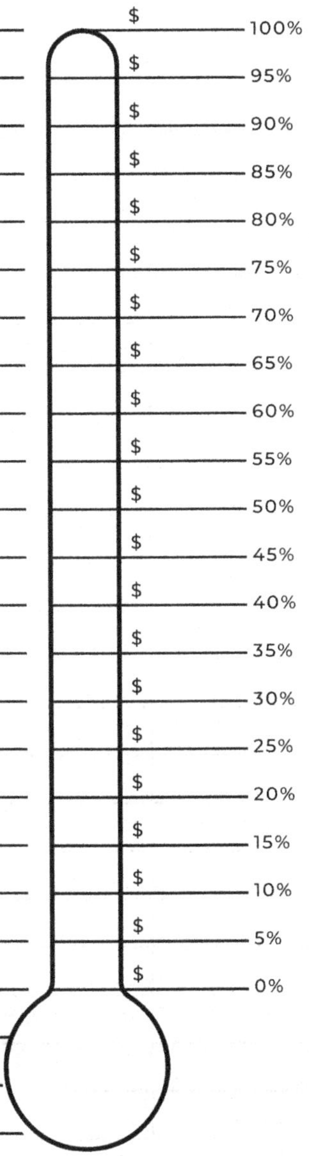

DEBT PAYOFF TRACKER

CREDITOR OR CONSOLIDATED LOAN

ACCOUNT #

ACCOUNT BALANCE

MONTHLY DUE DATE

INTEREST RATE

GOAL PAYOFF DATE

MINIMUM PAYMENT

DATE	PAYMENT MADE	BALANCE	NOTES

VISUAL PAYOFF PROGRESS

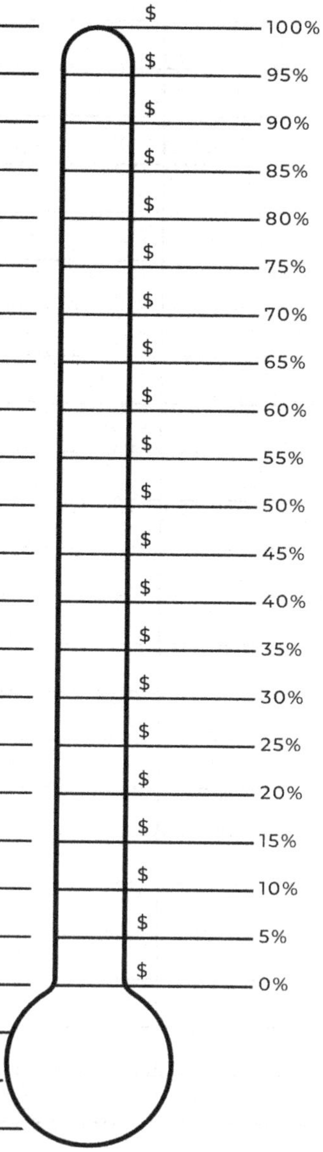

Managing Credit Utilization After Debt Consolidation

Credit utilization refers to the amount of credit you're using compared to your total available credit, and it's one of the most important factors in determining your credit score. It typically accounts for about 30% of your FICO score, which makes it a key area to focus on after debt consolidation. When you consolidate debt, whether through a personal loan, a balance transfer card, or other methods, your credit utilization ratio can change. Managing it properly will help you maintain or even improve your credit score.

What Is Credit Utilization?

Credit utilization is the ratio of your total outstanding credit card balances to your total credit card limits. For example, if you have a total credit limit of $10,000 across all your credit cards and your total balance is $3,000, your credit utilization is 30%.

Debt consolidation can affect your credit utilization in both positive and negative ways, depending on how you manage your credit afterward.

Let's take a closer look at what happens in different debt consolidation scenarios.

CONTINUE TO NEXT PAGE

PAYING OFF CREDIT CARD DEBT WITH A LOAN

If you consolidate your credit card debt into a personal loan, your credit utilization ratio will likely improve. Since credit utilization only considers revolving credit (such as credit cards), paying off your credit card balances brings your credit utilization to zero. Your new loan is considered installment credit, which doesn't factor into your credit utilization ratio.

Example: If you had $5,000 in credit card debt with a $10,000 limit (50% utilization), consolidating that into a loan will bring your utilization to 0%.

- **Managing Credit Utilization:** After consolidation, resist the temptation to run up new balances on the credit cards you just paid off. Keeping your cards open and at a $0 balance will have a positive impact on your credit score.

USING A BALANCE TRANSFER CARD

If you consolidate your debt using a balance transfer card, you'll transfer multiple high-interest credit card balances to a new card with a low or 0% introductory interest rate.

- **Positive Impact:** By transferring your balances to a single card, you can lower the overall interest you pay and potentially lower your credit utilization if the new card has a high credit limit.
- **Negative Impact:** If the new card's credit limit is lower than your combined original credit limits, your utilization ratio may increase, which can hurt your score. For example, if you transfer $5,000 in credit card debt to a card with a $6,000 limit, your utilization would be about 83%, which is very high.
- **Managing Credit Utilization:** When using a balance transfer, aim to pay off the transferred balance before the introductory rate expires. Keep your old cards open (with no balances) to avoid increasing your utilization.

CLOSING CREDIT CARDS AFTER CONSOLIDATION

One of the biggest mistakes people make after debt consolidation is closing the credit card accounts they've paid off. Closing these accounts can negatively impact your credit utilization ratio.

- **Negative Impact:** When you close credit cards, you reduce the total amount of credit available to you, which increases your utilization ratio if you still have balances on other cards.

Example: Let's say you had a $5,000 balance on a card with a $10,000 limit. After consolidation, if you close that card, you lose the $10,000 in available credit, which may increase your utilization ratio if you have remaining balances on other cards.

- **Managing Credit Utilization:** Keep your old credit card accounts open after consolidation, even if you're not using them. This will keep your total available credit higher and your utilization ratio lower.

EXPLORE BEST PRACTICES

Best Practices for Managing Credit Utilization After Debt Consolidation

Keep Credit Card Accounts Open

Even though you've paid off your credit cards through debt consolidation, keeping those accounts open is beneficial for your credit score. Here's why:

- **Lower Utilization:** Keeping your credit cards open with a $0 balance helps keep your total available credit higher, which lowers your credit utilization ratio.
- **Avoid Temptation:** While it's crucial to keep the accounts open, avoid using them unless absolutely necessary. This helps prevent accumulating new debt.

Avoid New Credit Card Debt

One of the dangers of debt consolidation is that once your credit cards are paid off, you may feel tempted to use them again. This could result in racking up new debt while still paying off the consolidation loan.

Action: *Create a spending plan that allows you to live within your means and avoid using credit cards for new purchases unless you can pay the balance in full each month.*

Best Practices for Managing Credit Utilization After Debt Consolidation

Monitor Your Credit Utilization Regularly
It's important to keep an eye on your credit utilization after consolidation to make sure it stays within a healthy range. Credit utilization below 30% is ideal for maintaining a good credit score, but keeping it as low as possible (e.g., under 10%) is even better.

Action: *Use credit monitoring services or check your credit report periodically to ensure your credit utilization ratio is staying low. You can also calculate your utilization manually by comparing your total balances to your total credit limit.*

Pay More Than the Minimum Payment
If you've consolidated your debt into a personal loan or balance transfer card, make it a goal to pay more than the minimum monthly payment.

Action: *By making extra payments, you'll reduce the total amount you owe faster, which helps you avoid accumulating new debt and ensures you pay off your consolidation loan in a shorter time.*

What Happens If You Don't Manage Credit Utilization After Consolidation?

If you don't manage your credit utilization properly after debt consolidation, several negative outcomes can occur:

- **Increased Credit Utilization:** Closing credit card accounts or running up new balances can quickly lead to higher credit utilization, hurting your credit score.
- **Accumulating More Debt:** If you use your newly paid-off credit cards without a repayment plan, you could end up with even more debt than before consolidation.
- **Higher Interest Costs:** If you transfer balances to a card with a low introductory rate but fail to pay it off before the promotional period ends, you may face high interest charges again.

Final Tips for Managing Credit Utilization

Stay Below 30% Utilization: Aim to keep your credit utilization ratio below 30% at all times. The lower your utilization, the better it is for your credit score.

Automate Payments: Set up automatic payments for your consolidation loan or balance transfer card to ensure you never miss a payment and keep your balances under control.

Use Cash or Debit for Expenses: Instead of relying on credit cards, switch to cash or debit for everyday purchases to prevent running up your balances again.

By effectively managing your credit utilization after debt consolidation, you can protect your credit score and make steady progress toward financial freedom.

MONTHLY RECAP

MONTH OF

THIS MONTH'S ACHIEVEMENTS

WHAT DO YOU FEEL WORKED THIS MONTH?

WHAT DO YOU FEEL DIDN'T WORK THIS MONTH?

THINGS TO DO MORE OF

MONTHLY GRATITUDE

Money TALK$

SAVINGS CHALLENGE + PAYCHECK POWER BOOSTER®

SECTION SEVEN

MONTHLY PLANNER

MONTH & YEAR

SUN	MON	TUE	WED	THU	FRI	SAT

TO DO:

THIS MONTH'S GOALS

MONTHLY AFFIRMATIONS

POSITIVE AFFIRMATION

I AM

empowered to achieve my financial dreams.

Overview of the Paycheck Power® Booster® Calculator Tool

The Paycheck Power® Booster® Calculator tool by Advantage Publications is a unique financial calculator that helps you understand how small, everyday purchases can add up over time and potentially interfere with long-term savings goals. It allows you to see how cutting back on "little things" (like a daily coffee or dining out) can lead to significant savings. The tool visually demonstrates how reallocating those funds can help boost your paycheck's potential and contribute toward important financial goals, such as emergency savings or retirement.

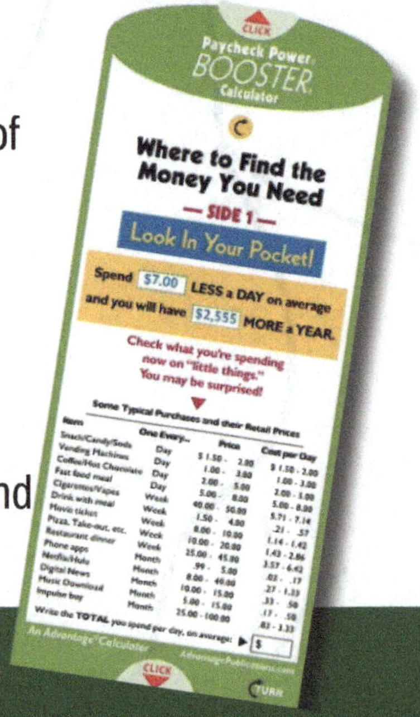

By providing clear insights on the impact of impulse spending, the Paycheck Power® Booster® Calculator tool helps you make smarter decisions about discretionary spending versus saving. As a seamless component of the **Money TALK$™ Financial Empowerment Tool Kit**, it reinforces spending plans, goal-setting, and long-term financial planning.

52-Week Saving$ Challenge

To complement the Paycheck Power® Booster® Calculator Tool, we've designed a 52-Week Savings Challenge that helps you consistently save money every week for an entire year. The challenge encourages you to gradually increase your savings, with specific weekly goals.

At the end of 52 weeks, you'll have built up a significant savings cushion!

52-WEEK SAVING$ CHALLENGE

Goal: Save a set amount each week starting small and increasing as the weeks progress.

Reflection: After each month, take a moment to reflect on your savings habits, what worked well, and areas for improvement.

WEEK	AMOUNT TO SAVE ($7,150 GOAL)	CUMULATIVE SAVINGS ($7,150 GOAL)	WEEK	AMOUNT TO SAVE ($7,150 GOAL)	CUMULATIVE SAVINGS ($7,150 GOAL)
1	$10	$10	18	$95	$945
2	$15	$25	19	$100	$1,045
3	$20	$45	20	$105	$1,150
4	$25	$70	21	$110	$1,260
5	$30	$100	22	$115	$1,375
6	$35	$135	23	$120	$1,495
7	$40	$175	24	$125	$1,620
8	$45	$220	25	$130	$1,750
9	$50	$270	26	$135	$1,885
10	$55	$325	27	$140	$2,025
11	$60	$385	28	$145	$2,170
12	$65	$450	29	$150	$2,320
13	$70	$520	30	$155	$2,475
14	$75	$595	31	$160	$2,635
15	$80	$675	32	$165	$2,800
16	$85	$760	33	$170	$2,970
17	$90	$850	34	$175	$3,145

52-WEEK SAVING$ CHALLENGE

Goal: Save a set amount each week starting small and increasing as the weeks progress.

Reflection: After each month, take a moment to reflect on your savings habits, what worked well, and areas for improvement.

WEEK	AMOUNT TO SAVE ($7,150 GOAL)	CUMULATIVE SAVINGS ($7,150 GOAL)
35	$180	$3,325
36	$185	$3,510
37	$190	$3,700
38	$195	$3,895
39	$200	$4,095
40	$205	$4,300
41	$210	$4,510
42	$215	$4,725
43	$220	$4,945

WEEK	AMOUNT TO SAVE ($7,150 GOAL)	CUMULATIVE SAVINGS ($7,150 GOAL)
44	$225	$5,170
45	$230	$5,400
46	$235	$5,635
47	$240	$5,875
48	$245	$6,120
49	$250	$6,370
50	$255	$6,625
51	$260	$6,885
52	$265	$7,150

By the end of 52 weeks, you will have saved $7,150!

"BEAT THE STATISTICS"

Goal: Beat the statistics by saving $1,430 in one year! Save a set amount each week by starting small and increasing as the weeks progress.

WEEK	AMOUNT TO SAVE ($1,430 GOAL)	CUMULATIVE SAVINGS ($1,430 GOAL)
1	$2	$2
2	$3	$5
3	$4	$9
4	$5	$14
5	$6	$20
6	$7	$27
7	$8	$35
8	$9	$44
9	$10	$54
10	$11	$65
11	$12	$77
12	$13	$90
13	$14	$104
14	$15	$119
15	$16	$135
16	$17	$152
17	$18	$170

WEEK	AMOUNT TO SAVE ($7,150 GOAL)	CUMULATIVE SAVINGS ($7,150 GOAL)
18	$19	$189
19	$20	$209
20	$21	$230
21	$22	$252
22	$23	$275
23	$24	$299
24	$25	$324
25	$26	$350
26	$27	$377
27	$28	$405
28	$29	$434
29	$30	$464
30	$31	$495
31	$32	$527
32	$33	$560
33	$34	$594
34	$35	$629

52-WEEK SAVING$ CHALLENGE

Goal: Save a set amount each week starting small and increasing as the weeks progress.

Reflection: After each month, take a moment to reflect on your savings habits, what worked well, and areas for improvement.

WEEK	AMOUNT TO SAVE ($7,150 GOAL)	CUMULATIVE SAVINGS ($7,150 GOAL)
35	$36	$665
36	$37	$702
37	$38	$740
38	$39	$779
39	$40	$819
40	$41	$860
41	$42	$902
42	$43	$945
43	$44	$989

WEEK	AMOUNT TO SAVE ($7,150 GOAL)	CUMULATIVE SAVINGS ($7,150 GOAL)
44	$45	$1,034
45	$46	$1,080
46	$47	$1,127
47	$48	$1,175
48	$49	$1,224
49	$50	$1,274
50	$51	$1,325
51	$52	$1,377
52	$53	$1,430

By the end of 52 weeks, you will have saved $1,430 which ensures you can handle a $1,000 emergency!

JOURNAL ENTRY

Date:

How does knowing I can handle a $1,000 emergency make me feel about my financial security?

Am I finding it easy or difficult to save? If so, why?

What changes did I make in my daily spending that helped me save more?

How do I feel about reaching my savings goal this month?

"A goal without a plan is just a wish."
— Antoine de Saint-Exupéry

MONTHLY RECAP

MONTH OF

THIS MONTH'S ACHIEVEMENTS

WHAT DO YOU FEEL WORKED THIS MONTH?

WHAT DO YOU FEEL DIDN'T WORK THIS MONTH?

THINGS TO DO MORE OF

MONTHLY GRATITUDE

Money TALK$

GROWING YOUR ASSETS

SECTION EIGHT

MONTHLY PLANNER

MONTH & YEAR

SUN	MON	TUE	WED	THU	FRI	SAT

TO DO:

THIS MONTH'S GOALS

MONTHLY AFFIRMATIONS

POSITIVE AFFIRMATION

I AM
free from limiting beliefs about money.

Money TALK$

Growing Assets

Building and **growing assets** is a crucial part of achieving long-term financial security and wealth. Assets are resources that have economic value and can help you generate income or appreciate in value over time. This guide will walk you through identifying, acquiring, and growing various types of assets, as well as providing a structured checklist for tracking your current and future assets.

Identifying Assets

Assets are divided into different categories, and each type plays a unique role in building wealth. Here are some common asset types:

Real Estate
Real estate includes land, residential homes, commercial properties, and rental properties. Investing in real estate can generate rental income and appreciate over time.

Home Ownership
Owning your home is often one of the largest assets people have. As you pay off your mortgage, you build equity, which increases your net worth.

Stocks:
When you buy shares of a company, you own a piece of that company. Stocks tend to appreciate over time, and many companies offer dividends.

Bonds
Bonds are loans made to corporations or governments. They are generally more stable than stocks, providing fixed interest payments over time.

Mutual Funds and ETFs
These are collections of stocks and bonds, which allow you to diversify your investments and reduce risk.

Retirement Accounts
Contributing to retirement accounts like a 401(k), IRA, or Roth IRA can grow your wealth over time with tax advantages. Employers may also match contributions, further boosting your investments.

Growing Assets

Emergency Fund
A well-funded emergency account (typically 3-6 months of living expenses) is a foundational asset that provides financial security.

High-Yield Savings Accounts These accounts offer higher interest rates than traditional savings accounts, allowing your money to grow faster with minimal risk.

Owning a Business
If you own a business, it is considered an asset because it generates income and can increase in value over time. Whether it's a side hustle or a full-time endeavor, owning a business is a powerful wealth-building tool.

Investing in Businesses
If you're not ready to start your own business, you can invest in other people's businesses through venture capital or equity crowdfunding.

Trademarks, Patents, and Copyrights
These are forms of intellectual property that can generate income through licensing or royalties. For example, if you write a book, own a patent, or trademark a product, these can become valuable assets that provide passive income.

Growing Assets

Once you have identified your assets, the next step is to actively grow them. Here are some strategies for expanding your asset portfolio:

Leverage Compound Interest

Albert Einstein reportedly said, "Compound interest is the eighth wonder of the world. He who understands it, earns it; he who doesn't, pays it." Compound interest allows your assets to grow exponentially over time. The earlier you start investing or saving, the more powerful this effect becomes.

Maximize Tax-Advantaged Accounts

Take full advantage of accounts like **401(k)s** or **IRAs** that offer tax-deferred or tax-free growth. This allows you to keep more of your money growing in the market, rather than losing a portion of it to taxes.

Diversify Your Investments

Don't put all your eggs in one basket. A diversified portfolio spreads your investments across different asset classes (stocks, bonds, real estate, etc.), reducing risk and increasing the likelihood of steady growth.

Reinvest Profits

Whether it's dividends from stocks or rental income from property, reinvesting profits rather than spending them can accelerate your wealth-building process. The longer you leave your money in, the more it compounds.

Protect Your Assets

Don't put all your eggs in one basket. A diversified portfolio spreads your investments across different asset classes (stocks, bonds, real estate, etc.), reducing risk and increasing the likelihood of steady growth.

THE WEALTH FORMULA

Wealth-building is not just about money, but also about time and managing other financial factors like inflation and interest. Here's a simple formula that captures this:

WEALTH = MONEY + TIME +/– RATE OF RETURN – INFLATION - TAXES

MONEY
Your earnings, savings, and investments.

INFLATION
Inflation erodes purchasing power over time, so your investments need to outpace inflation.

TIME
The longer your money is invested, the more it grows (thanks to compound interest).

TAXES
Mandatory financial charges imposed by the government on individuals and businesses to fund public services such as infrastructure, education, and healthcare.

Tracking current and future assets is crucial for ensuring financial growth and stability. By keeping a detailed record, you can identify trends, make informed decisions, and plan for future investments.

Monitoring your assets helps you stay on top of your financial health and avoid potential losses. To assist you in this process, we invite you to utilize our **Asset Tracking Checklist.**

Asset Tracking Checklist

Current Assets

	ASSET	DESCRIPTION	CURRENT VALUE
	Home Equity	Current value of your home minus any mortgage balance	$
	Savings Account(s)	Emergency fund, high-yield savings, etc.	$
	Retirement Account(s)	Total balance and contributions of 401k, IRAs, etc. accounts	$
	Stock Portfolio	Total value of your stocks and mutual funds	$
	Bonds	Current value of any bonds or bond funds	$
	Real Estate Investments	Value of rental properties or land	$
	Intellectual Property	Royalties, licensing income, etc.	$
	Business(es)	Value of your business or side hustle	$
	Other Assets	Any additional investments or valuable possessions	$

Future Asset Goals

- Increase Retirement Savings by $_________________ (Contribution Goal)
- Save $_____________ for a down payment on a rental property
- Diversify portfolio by adding bonds, real estate or alternative investments
- Start or invest in a new business
- Build an emergency fund of $____________________
- Maximize contributions to tax-advantaged accounts

How to Minimize Investment Risks

Minimizing investment risks is key to preserving and growing your wealth, especially when navigating uncertain markets. Here are some strategies to help reduce risk while still achieving growth:

1. Diversify Your Portfolio

Why It Works: *Diversification means spreading your investments across different asset classes, industries, and geographic regions to reduce risk. This way, poor performance in one area can be offset by better performance in another.*

How to Apply: Hold a mix of stocks, bonds, real estate, and cash. Additionally, within stocks, invest in various sectors like technology, healthcare, and consumer goods, as well as in both domestic and international markets.

2. Invest for the Long Term

Why It Works: *The longer you stay invested, the more time your assets have to recover from short-term volatility. Historically, markets tend to rise over the long term, even after downturns.*

How to Apply: *Choose investments that align with your long-term financial goals (e.g., retirement) and avoid trying to time the market by making frequent trades based on short- term market movements.*

3. Dollar-Cost Averaging

Why It Works: *Dollar-cost averaging (DCA) involves investing a fixed amount of money at regular intervals, regardless of market conditions. This strategy reduces the risk of investing a large sum in a market peak and allows you to take advantage of lower prices when markets dip.*

How to Apply: *Set up automatic contributions to your retirement accounts or investment funds on a monthly or quarterly basis. This smooths out the average cost of your investments over time.*

How to Minimize Investment Risks - Continued

4. Keep an Emergency Fund
Why It Works: *Having a well-funded emergency account reduces the need to liquidate investments in case of unexpected expenses, thus protecting your portfolio during downturns.*

How to Apply: *Keep 3-6 months of living expenses in a high-yield savings account to cover emergencies like job loss or medical bills.*

5. Rebalance Your Portfolio
Why It Works: *Over time, the performance of different assets can cause your portfolio to drift from your desired asset allocation. Rebalancing brings your portfolio back in line with your original risk tolerance and investment strategy.*

How to Apply: *Periodically (e.g., annually or semi-annually) review your portfolio and sell portions of over-performing assets while buying more of under-performing assets to maintain your target allocation.*

6. Understand Your Risk Tolerance
Why It Works: *Different investments come with different levels of risk. Understanding your personal risk tolerance helps you choose investments that match your comfort level and financial goals.*

How to Apply: *Assess how much volatility you're willing to accept. If market fluctuations make you anxious, consider a more conservative portfolio with a higher allocation to bonds or cash equivalents.*

How to Minimize Investment Risks - Continued

7. Stay Informed but Avoid Overreacting

Why It Works: *Staying informed about market trends, economic indicators, and your investments is crucial. However, reacting to short-term news or market fluctuations can lead to poor decision-making and increased risk.*

How to Apply: *Stay updated with reliable financial news, but avoid making impulsive decisions based on market hype or fear. Stick to your long-term plan.*

8. Invest in Low-Cost Index Funds or ETFs

Why It Works: *Index funds and exchange-traded funds (ETFs) allow you to invest in a broad market segment, which reduces individual stock risk. Additionally, they typically have lower fees than actively managed funds, which can save you money over time.*

How to Apply: *Consider allocating a portion of your portfolio to low-cost index funds or ETFs that track major indices like the S&P 500. These funds provide diversification at a low cost.*

9. Avoid High-Risk Investments

Why It Works: *High-risk investments, like penny stocks or speculative cryptocurrencies, can lead to significant losses. While these may offer high potential rewards, they often come with the risk of total loss.*

How to Apply: *Limit exposure to highly speculative investments to a small percentage of your portfolio (5-10%), and ensure the bulk of your assets are in more stable, established investments.*

How to Minimize Investment Risks - Continued

10. Hedge Against Inflation

Why It Works: *Inflation erodes the purchasing power of your money, so it's important to invest in assets that can grow faster than inflation. Over time, inflation can significantly reduce the real value of your savings.*

How to Apply: *Consider investing in assets that have historically outpaced inflation, such as stocks, real estate, or Treasury Inflation-Protected Securities (TIPS).*

By incorporating these strategies, you can minimize the risks associated with investing while still positioning yourself for growth and financial success. Remember, reducing risk doesn't mean eliminating it—some risk is necessary to achieve returns, but smart strategies can help you manage it effectively.

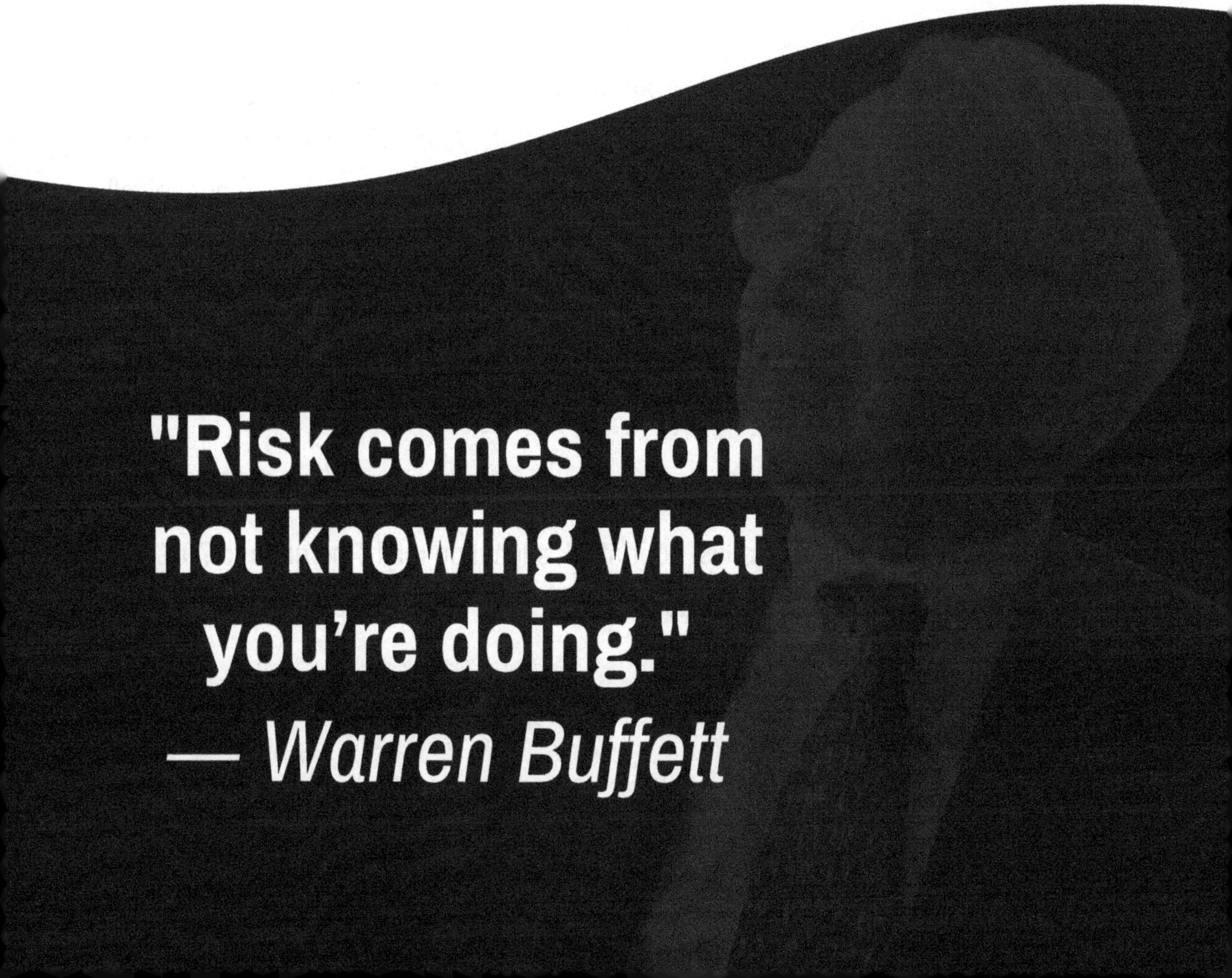

Asset Allocation Strategies

Asset allocation is the process of dividing your investment portfolio among different asset classes, such as stocks, bonds, real estate, and cash, based on your financial goals, risk tolerance, and investment timeline. The goal is to balance risk and reward by allocating assets in a way that aligns with your specific financial objectives.

Here's an overview of asset allocation strategies and how they work:

Strategic Asset Allocation

Strategic asset allocation is a long-term approach where you set target percentages for each asset class and periodically rebalance your portfolio to maintain those targets.

How It Works: Based on your risk tolerance and investment goals, you might choose to allocate, for example, 60% to stocks, 30% to bonds, and 10% to real estate. Over time, market fluctuations may cause your allocations to drift, so you would periodically rebalance the portfolio back to these target percentages.

Best For: Long-term investors who want to stick to a consistent, disciplined strategy. This approach doesn't involve frequent changes and focuses on the long-term growth of your portfolio.

Example: If the stock market grows, your stock allocation might increase to 70%. You would sell some stocks and buy bonds or other assets to rebalance back to the 60/30/10 mix.

Tactical Asset Allocation

Tactical asset allocation allows for short-term deviations from your strategic allocation to take advantage of market conditions. It's a more flexible approach than strategic allocation.

How It Works: While you maintain a long-term target allocation, you temporarily overweight or underweight certain asset classes when you see market opportunities. For instance, if you expect stocks to perform well in the short term, you might increase your stock allocation from 60% to 70%, with plans to revert to your original allocation once the market opportunity passes.

Best For: Investors who are comfortable with a more hands-on approach and are knowledgeable about market trends. This strategy requires a greater understanding of market conditions and timing.

Growth vs. Income Asset Allocation

This strategy balances growth-oriented assets like stocks with income-oriented assets like bonds or dividend-paying investments, based on your financial goals.

Growth Allocation: Typically, growth portfolios are heavy in stocks, which have higher potential for capital appreciation but also come with higher risk. Younger investors or those with a longer time horizon often adopt this strategy because they can afford to ride out market volatility.

Income Allocation: Investors looking for income rather than capital appreciation may allocate more toward bonds, dividend-paying stocks, and real estate, which generate regular income but tend to be less volatile. This strategy is ideal for retirees or those close to retirement who need steady income rather than aggressive growth.

Best For: Individuals focused on achieving either capital growth or income, depending on their life stage and financial goals.

Risk-Based Asset Allocation

This strategy aligns your asset allocation directly with your risk tolerance. There are typically three levels of risk-based portfolios: conservative, moderate, and aggressive.

- **Conservative Allocation:** A conservative portfolio is designed for risk-averse investors and typically includes a larger proportion of bonds and cash. A typical allocation might be 20% stocks, 60% bonds, and 20% cash. This minimizes volatility but also offers lower potential returns.
- **Moderate Allocation:** For those with a moderate risk tolerance, the portfolio may be more balanced between stocks and bonds, such as a 60% stock and 40% bond mix. This approach offers a blend of growth potential with some downside protection.
- **Aggressive Allocation:** An aggressive portfolio focuses on maximizing growth by investing primarily in stocks (e.g., 80-90% stocks). This is suitable for investors with a high-risk tolerance who can weather market swings in exchange for the potential for higher returns.

Age-Based Asset Allocation (Lifecycle Approach)

This approach adjusts your asset allocation as you age. The younger you are, the more heavily weighted your portfolio will be toward growth assets like stocks. As you approach retirement, the portfolio gradually shifts toward more conservative, income-generating assets like bonds.

How It Works: A common rule of thumb is the "100 minus age" rule: subtract your age from 100 to determine the percentage of your portfolio that should be in stocks. For example, if you're 30, 70% of your portfolio should be in stocks and 30% in bonds. As you age, the allocation shifts to more bonds and fewer stocks to reduce risk.

Best For: Investors who want their portfolios to adjust automatically based on their life stage. Many target-date retirement funds use this type of asset allocation strategy.

Dynamic Asset Allocation

In dynamic asset allocation, you constantly adjust your portfolio based on market conditions and your personal financial situation. It is more flexible than strategic or tactical asset allocation because it allows for frequent changes.

How It Works: You may increase or decrease exposure to certain asset classes based on market conditions or life changes, such as a shift in your financial goals or the economy. For example, in a recession, you might move more into bonds, while in a bull market, you could shift more into stocks.

Best For: Investors who want to actively manage their portfolios and have the time and knowledge to make frequent adjustments based on changing market conditions.

Core-Satellite Asset Allocation

This strategy combines a core investment that makes up the majority of your portfolio with satellite investments that are used to enhance returns or reduce risk.

How It Works: The core of your portfolio is typically made up of low-cost, broad-based index funds (e.g., an S&P 500 index fund), while satellite investments might include specific stocks, sector funds, or international investments to add diversification and potential growth.

Best For: Investors who want a stable foundation in their portfolio (the core) while still having some flexibility to pursue higher-risk opportunities with a smaller portion of their investments (the satellites).

Important Considerations in Asset Allocation

Rebalancing: No matter what strategy you choose, it's important to rebalance your portfolio periodically. Rebalancing means returning your portfolio to its original asset allocation by selling overperforming assets and buying underperforming ones. This helps you maintain the risk level you're comfortable with.

Risk Tolerance: Your risk tolerance will determine the appropriate mix of assets for your portfolio. Risk tolerance is influenced by factors such as age, income stability, investment knowledge, and personal financial goals.

Time Horizon: The longer your time horizon, the more risk you can afford to take. For example, someone investing for retirement 30 years from now can afford to have more of their portfolio in stocks, while someone retiring in five years may want to shift more toward bonds to preserve capital.

JOURNAL ENTRY

Date:

What assets (such as property, investments, or even skills) do you currently have that you might be undervaluing?

How can you invest more in these to grow your wealth over time?

"Diversification is the only free lunch in finance."
— Harry Markowitz, Nobel Laureate in Economic Sciences

MONTHLY RECAP

MONTH OF

THIS MONTH'S ACHIEVEMENTS

WHAT DO YOU FEEL WORKED THIS MONTH?

WHAT DO YOU FEEL DIDN'T WORK THIS MONTH?

THINGS TO DO MORE OF

MONTHLY GRATITUDE

Money TALK$

LEVERAGING ASSETS

SECTION NINE

MONTHLY PLANNER

MONTH & YEAR

SUN	MON	TUE	WED	THU	FRI	SAT

TO DO:

THIS MONTH'S GOALS

MONTHLY AFFIRMATIONS

POSITIVE AFFIRMATION

I AM

grateful for every step I take toward my goals.

Money TALK$

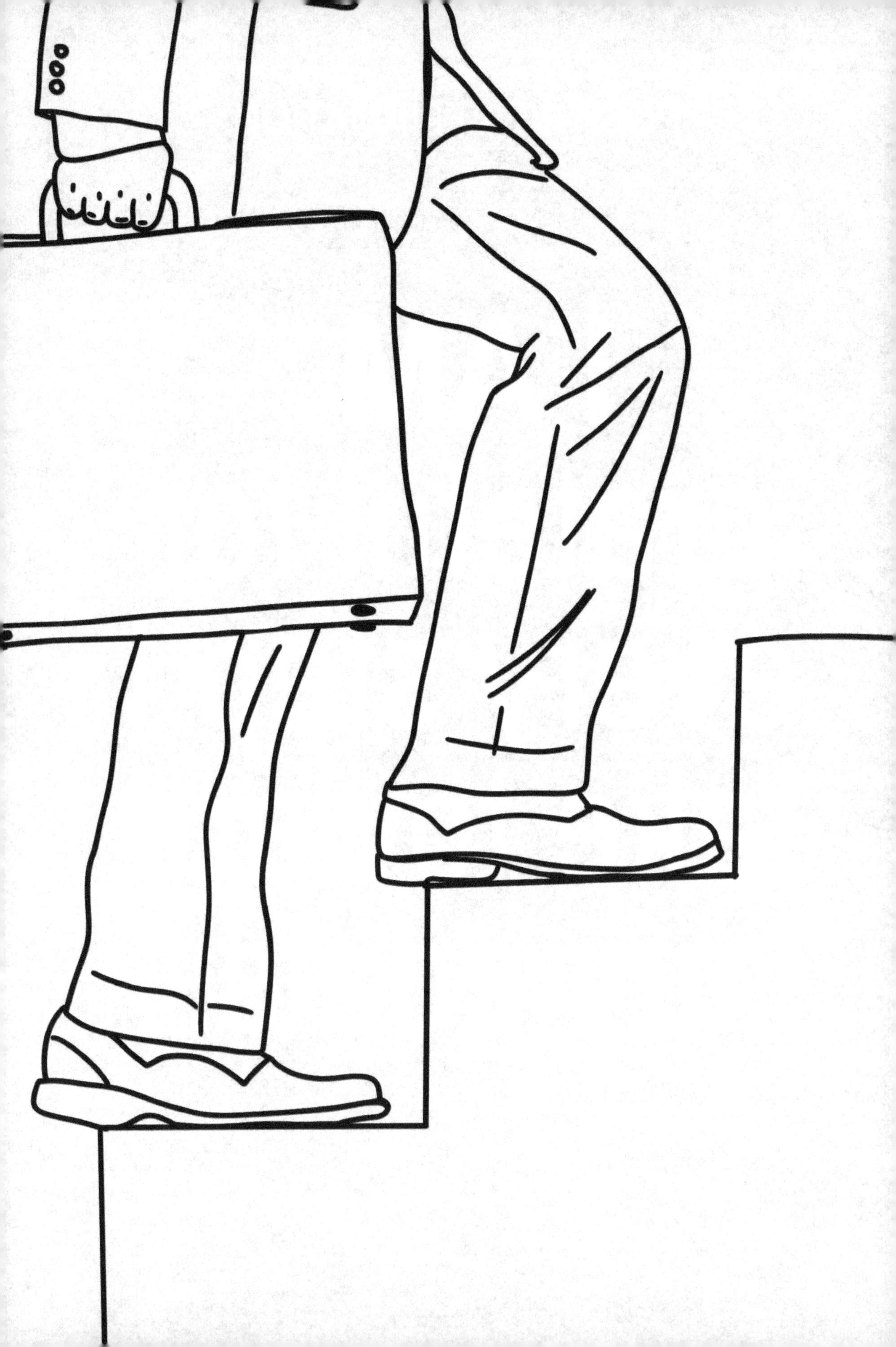

Simplifying "Leveraging"

In finance, leverage means using existing resources (or borrowed money) to increase the potential return on an investment. Simply put, it's like using something you already own to gain more value or income from it.

For example, if you own a property and take out a loan using that property as collateral to invest in something else, you're leveraging that property. The idea is to use your assets to amplify your ability to generate more wealth. However, leverage also comes with risks. If the investment doesn't perform as expected, you may still be responsible for repaying any borrowed funds, so it's important to leverage wisely.

Strategies for Leveraging Assets to Generate Additional Income

Leverage Real Estate for Rental Income

How It Works: If you own property, you can leverage it by renting it out. This creates a steady stream of passive income, which can be reinvested or used to pay down the mortgage.

Action Steps:

- Determine if your property can be rented.
- Research rental market rates in your area.
- List your property for rent or explore short-term rental platforms like Airbnb.
- Use rental income to cover costs or reinvest.

Use Investment Leverage

How It Works: Many investors use leverage by borrowing money (often through margin trading) to invest in stocks, real estate, or other assets. The borrowed money allows you to increase your potential returns, but also increases the risk of losses.

Action Steps:

- Consult a financial advisor about margin trading or leveraging investments.
- Borrow conservatively and focus on stable investments.
- Set clear targets for when to pay off borrowed amounts.

Simplifying "Leveraging" - Continued

Leveraging Business Assets

How It Works: If you own a business, you can leverage business assets (like equipment or inventory) to secure loans that fund business growth, expansion, or new investments.

Action Steps:

- Evaluate your business assets to determine their borrowing power.
- Apply for a business loan using these assets as collateral.
- Use the loan to grow or scale your business, improving overall income.

Borrowing Against Life Insurance Policies

How It Works: Whole life and universal life insurance (fixed, indexed and/or variable) policies build cash value over time. You can borrow against this value for other investments or expenses.

Action Steps:

- Review your life insurance policy to determine if it builds cash value.
- Borrow against the policy, keeping in mind the interest charged on the loan.
- Use the borrowed amount for investments or paying down higher-interest debts.

Leveraging Intellectual Property (IP)

How It Works: If you own intellectual property, such as trademarks, patents, or copyrights, you can license these assets to others in exchange for royalties.

Action Steps:

- Identify valuable IP assets (patents, brands, trademarks).
- Research licensing opportunities in your industry.
- Enter into licensing agreements to generate passive income.

Checklist for Leveraging Assets

Real Estate

Determine property value.

Research rental income potential.

Set up short-term or long-term rental options.

Explore home equity loans or refinancing options for reinvestment.

Investments

Identify investment accounts that allow margin or leverage.

Calculate safe leverage ratios.

Borrow strategically to invest in diversified assets.

Business Assets

Evaluate equipment, property, or inventory for collateral use.

Apply for business loans to scale operations.

Life Insurance

Review policy's cash value.

Calculate how much you can borrow without affecting coverage.

Intellectual Property

Inventory IP assets (patents, trademarks, copyrights).

Explore potential licensing deals.

Set up royalty agreements for passive income.

Asset-Leverage Plan Worksheet

Understanding leveraging and having a plan for it is important for growing your finances and managing risks. Leveraging lets you use borrowed money or other tools to make more from your investments. But it also comes with risks that can affect your financial stability if not handled well. A good leveraging plan helps you use your assets wisely to make extra income while keeping risks under control.

Example: How Leverage Works

Here's a simple example illustrating how leverage amplifies potential gains (and risks):

Your Asset: Property valued at $100,000
Leverage: Borrow $50,000 against the property
Invest: Use the $50,000 to purchase stocks or start a business
Outcome: Generate income from the investment (potential gains) while maintaining ownership of the property

Create Your Asset-Leveraging Plan

Step 1: Identify Your Assets: (Property, Investments, Business, etc.)
Step 2: Explore Leverage Options: (Renting Property, Loans, etc.)
Step 3: Set Income Goals: (How much addt'l income can this make?)
Step 4: Take Action: (Follow through with actionable steps and track.)

We are providing an Asset-Leveraging Plan worksheet to track your leveraging activities and maintain a balanced approach.

Asset-Leverage Plan Worksheet

ASSET	LEVERAGE STRATEGY	EXPECTED INCOME	ACTION STEPS	PROGRESS/ TIMELINE
Real Estate Property	Rental Income	$2,500/mo	Research rental prices in the area & find tenants	6 months

ALWAYS TAKE INTO ACCOUNT YOUR RISK TOLERANCE AND FINANCIAL SITUATION BEFORE ENGAGING IN LEVERAGE.

Disclaimer: This information is provided for educational purposes only and is not intended to be individual financial, real estate, insurance, nor investment advice. The strategies and approaches discussed may not be suitable for everyone, and individual financial situations can vary. Always consult a **licensed financial advisor**, insurance, investment and/or lending professional for personalized advice tailored to your financial circumstances and goals.

MONTHLY RECAP

MONTH OF

THIS MONTH'S ACHIEVEMENTS

WHAT DO YOU FEEL WORKED THIS MONTH?

WHAT DO YOU FEEL DIDN'T WORK THIS MONTH?

THINGS TO DO MORE OF

MONTHLY GRATITUDE

Money TALK$

PROTECTING ASSETS

SECTION TEN

MONTHLY PLANNER

MONTH & YEAR

SUN	MON	TUE	WED	THU	FRI	SAT

TO DO:

THIS MONTH'S GOALS

MONTHLY AFFIRMATIONS

POSITIVE AFFIRMATION

I AM dedicated to making positive financial progress.

Money TALK$

What is Personal Asset Protection?

Personal asset protection refers to strategies and tools designed to shield your wealth from potential risks such as lawsuits, creditors, taxes, and unforeseen life events like illness or death. In layman's terms, it's about ensuring that the money, property, and investments you've worked hard to accumulate remain safe and intact—both for you and for the generations that follow.

The goal is to safeguard your assets so that they are preserved in the event of financial challenges or legal actions, and to ensure they can be passed on to heirs or used to maintain your quality of life in retirement.

CHECKLIST FOR PROTECTING **ASSETS**

Insurance

Health Insurance: Covers medical expenses and protects you from overwhelming healthcare costs.

Homeowner's or Renter's Insurance: Protects your property against damage from natural disasters, theft, or other accidents.

Life Insurance: Provides financial security to your family in the event of your death. Whole life insurance can also build cash value over time.

Disability Insurance: Ensures income if you are unable to work due to illness or injury.

Liability Insurance: Protects you from legal claims if someone is injured on your property or as a result of your actions (e.g., umbrella insurance).

Auto Insurance: Covers damages and liability associated with driving.

Long-Term Care Insurance: Helps cover the cost of care if you develop a condition that requires long-term assistance.

CHECKLIST FOR PROTECTING **ASSETS** - CONT.

Estate Planning

Will: A legal document that details how your assets will be distributed after your death.

Trust: A legal entity that holds and manages assets for beneficiaries. Trusts can help minimize estate taxes and avoid probate.

Power of Attorney: Grants someone authority to manage your financial affairs if you become unable to do so.

Healthcare Directive (Living Will): Outlines your medical wishes if you become incapacitated and unable to communicate.

Beneficiary Designations: Ensure that all your retirement accounts, life insurance policies, and other financial accounts have updated beneficiaries.

Financial Safeguards

Emergency Fund: Set aside 3-6 months of living expenses in a high-yield savings account to protect against unexpected financial shocks.

Asset Titling: Consider titling assets in a way that offers protection, such as joint tenancy with rights of survivorship, tenancy by the entirety (for married couples), or transferring assets into a trust.

Debt Reduction: Reducing or eliminating high-interest debt can protect your assets from creditors and help build a more stable financial future.

Diversification: Spread your investments across different asset classes (stocks, bonds, real estate) to reduce risk and protect your portfolio against market downturns.

Retirement Accounts: Contribute to tax-advantaged retirement accounts like 401(k)s or IRAs. These accounts often have legal protections from creditors in many jurisdictions.

Creating a Plan for Safeguarding Wealth for Future Generations

Money TALK$ FACT

Protecting your wealth for the long term involves thoughtful planning and active management.

Below is a guide for creating a structured plan to ensure your assets are protected and can be passed on to your heirs:

Step 1: Inventory Your Assets

- Make a list of all your assets, including real estate, investment accounts, businesses, personal property, intellectual property, and other valuable possessions. Ensure all accounts and policies have updated beneficiaries.

Step 2: Set Up Legal Protections

- Create or update a **will** or **trust** to manage how assets will be distributed to heirs. Trusts can provide greater control and privacy over how assets are passed on, while reducing estate taxes.
- Review your **beneficiary designations** on retirement accounts, life insurance, and investment accounts to ensure they reflect your current wishes.

Step 3: Address Tax Considerations

- Consider working with a financial advisor or estate planner to explore **tax-saving strategies**. Trusts, gifting, or transferring assets during your lifetime can help minimize the tax burden on your heirs.
- Use **tax-advantaged accounts** like 529 plans for education savings or retirement accounts to pass wealth on more efficiently.

Step 4: Protect Against Legal Risks

- Explore **liability protection** options like umbrella insurance to shield your personal wealth from lawsuits or other legal claims.
- Consider **asset protection trusts** in some states that can shield assets from creditors.

Step 5: Communicate with Family

- Discuss your plans with your family or heirs to ensure they understand your wishes and can manage the assets properly when the time comes.

Asset-Protection Plan Worksheet

ASSET	PROTECTION STRATEGY	ACTION STEPS	TARGET DATE
Real Estate	Homeowner's Insurance & Trust	Set up trust for property	Q2 2025

Disclaimer: This information is provided for educational purposes only and is not intended to be individual financial, real estate, insurance, nor investment advice. The strategies and approaches discussed may not be suitable for everyone, and individual financial situations can vary. Always consult a **licensed financial advisor**, insurance, investment and/or lending professional for personalized advice tailored to your financial circumstances and goals.

MONTHLY RECAP

MONTH OF

THIS MONTH'S ACHIEVEMENTS

WHAT DO YOU FEEL WORKED THIS MONTH?

WHAT DO YOU FEEL DIDN'T WORK THIS MONTH?

THINGS TO DO MORE OF

MONTHLY GRATITUDE

Money
TALK$

FINANCIAL CONCEPTS CHEAT SHEETS

SECTION ELEVEN

MONTHLY PLANNER

MONTH & YEAR

SUN	MON	TUE	WED	THU	FRI	SAT

TO DO:

THIS MONTH'S GOALS

MONTHLY AFFIRMATIONS

POSITIVE AFFIRMATION

I CREATE opportunities for wealth and success.

Money TALKS

YEAR IN REVIEW

Financial Concepts Cheatsheets

Welcome to Your Financial Concepts Cheatsheets

Understanding money doesn't have to feel overwhelming. With the right tools and knowledge, you can simplify financial decisions and take confident steps toward building wealth. These seven key financial concepts are more than just ideas—they're your blueprint for financial empowerment.

This section is designed to:

- **Make complex concepts relatable and easy to apply.**
- **Help you take action that aligns with your goals and dreams.**
- **Strengthen your confidence when working with your financial advisor.**

Let's break down these concepts so you can use them to level up your financial wellbeing.

The Wealth Formula

THE WEALTH FORMULA

MONEY

+ TIME

+/- RATE OF RETURN

⊖ INFLATION

⊖ TAXES

WEALTH

Fair Use Disclaimer: This is a concept/goal developed by World Financial Group (WFG) and is used for illustrative and educational purposes only.

Source: https://www.facebook.com/share/196vpn9z7d/

What It Is:

This formula explains the building blocks of wealth:

Why It Matters:

- It highlights the factors you can control, like saving more or reducing your tax liability.

- It reminds you that time is your best ally in growing wealth.

Action Step:

Look at the formula as your personal strategy. What can you adjust—your savings rate, your investment choices, or your tax strategy—to accelerate your wealth-building journey?

Investment Decision Filter (PRTF)

What It Is:

A simple framework for evaluating investments through five lenses:

P

Performance: Does the investment perform consistently?

R

Risk: What level of risk does it carry, and does it align with your comfort zone?

T

Taxes: How will it impact your tax situation now and in the future?

F

Fees: Are the fees reasonable for the value provided?

• **Time/Emotional Investment: How much time or stress will managing this investment require?**

Why It Matters:

- It ensures your investments align with your financial goals and values.
- It reduces the emotional decision-making that often leads to mistakes.

Action Step:

Use this filter to assess potential investments and prioritize those that meet your needs.

The Rule of 72 (Compound Interest)

What It Is:

A simple way to estimate how long it takes your investment to double:

72 ÷ Interest Rate = Years to Double

Why It Matters:

- It shows how powerful compounding can be when you let your money work for you.
- It's a motivating reminder that consistent investing pays off over time.

Action Step:

Use the Rule of 72 to track the growth of your savings or investments. Then ask yourself: How can you maximize your rate of return to double your money faster?

THE RULE OF 72: COMPOUND INTEREST

How long before your $1,000 doubles?

Interest Rate	Doubling Time	EST. Savings
1%	72 Yrs	$2,047.10
3%	24 Yrs	$2,032.79
6%	12 Yrs	$2,012.20
8%	9 Yrs	$1,999.00
10%	7.2 Yrs	$2,143.59
11%	6.55 Yrs	$2,076.16
12%	6 Yrs	$1,973.82

Sequence of Returns Risk

What It Is:

The risk that poor investment returns early in retirement can significantly impact your savings.

Why It Matters:

- It highlights the importance of a withdrawal strategy for retirement.
- It teaches you to protect your assets during volatile markets.

Action Step:

Work with your advisor to create a diversified portfolio and plan for withdrawing money safely during retirement.

MS. HAPPY				
Year	Rate of Return	Beginning Value	Withdrawal	Ending Value
		$100,000		
1	30.00%	$130,000	$6,000	$124,000
2	20.00%	$148,800	$6,000	$142,800
3	10.00%	$157,080	$6,000	$151,080
4	10.00%	$166,188	$6,000	$160,188
5	10.00%	$176,207	$6,000	$170,207
6	10.00%	$187,227	$6,000	$181,227
7	10.00%	$199,350	$6,000	$193,350
8	10.00%	$212,685	$6,000	$206,685
9	-20.00%	$165,348	$6,000	$159,348
10	-30.00%	$111,544	$6,000	$105,544

MS. UNHAPPY				
Year	Rate of Return	Beginning Value	Withdrawal	Ending Value
		$100,000		
1	-30.00%	$70,000	$6,000	$64,000
2	-20.00%	$51,200	$6,000	$45,200
3	10.00%	$49,720	$6,000	$43,720
4	10.00%	$48,092	$6,000	$42,092
5	10.00%	$46,301	$6,000	$40,301
6	10.00%	$44,331	$6,000	$38,331
7	10.00%	$42,164	$6,000	$36,164
8	10.00%	$39,781	$6,000	$33,781
9	20.00%	$40,537	$6,000	$34,537
10	30.00%	$44,898	$6,000	$38,898

Fair Use Disclaimer: This is a concept was expressed by Whitney & Associates and is used for illustrative and educational purposes only. Source: https://whitneyandassociates.net/

Dollar Cost Averaging

What It Is:

An investment strategy where you invest a fixed amount regularly, regardless of market conditions.

Why It Matters:

- It removes the stress of trying to "time" the market.
- It allows you to take advantage of market fluctuations by buying more shares when prices are low.

Action Step:

Commit to consistent contributions into your investment accounts, like your 401(k) or Roth IRA, to build wealth steadily over time.

Month	Amount Invested	Price	Stocks Bought That Month	Total		Average Cost Price
				Stocks Bought	Amount Invested	
Jan	$100	$10.00	10.00	10.00	$100.00	$10.00
Feb	$100	$11.00	9.09	19.09	$200.00	$10.48
Mar	$100	$12.00	8.33	27.42	$300.00	$10.94
Apr	$100	$11.00	9.09	36.52	$400.00	$10.95
May	$100	$10.00	10.00	46.52	$500.00	$10.75
Jun	$100	$9.00	11.11	57.63	$600.00	$10.41
Jul	$100	$8.00	12.50	70.13	$700.00	$9.98
Aug	$100	$7.00	14.29	84.41	$800.00	$9.48
Sep	$100	$8.50	11.76	96.18	$900.00	$9.36
Oct	$100	$10.00	10.00	106.18	$1,000.00	$9.42
Nov	$100	$11.00	9.09	115.27	$1,100.00	$9.54
Dec	$100	$10.00	10.00	125.27	$1,200.00	$9.58

Fair Use Disclaimer: This is a concept expressed by Easy Peasy Finance and is used for illustrative and educational purposes only. https://www.easypeasyfinance.com/dollar-cost-averaging-for-kids-stocks-mf/

The 3-Legged Stool: Old vs. New

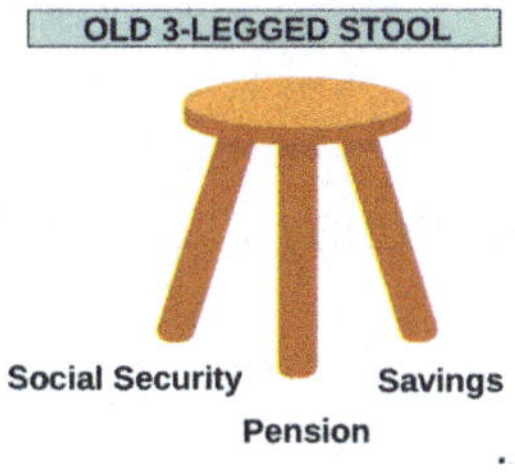

The Old 3-Legged Stool:

Traditionally, retirement income was supported by three main sources:

1. **Pension Plans:** Provided guaranteed income for life.
2. **Social Security:** Supplemented income in retirement.
3. **Personal Savings:** Funds individuals saved during their working years.

Why It's Outdated:

- Fewer employers offer pensions, leaving many retirees reliant on personal savings and Social Security.
- Rising costs and longer life expectancies have stretched the limits of these traditional pillars.

The New 3-Legged Stool:

Today, retirement income often comes from these diversified sources:

1. **Real Estate:** Income from rental properties or equity growth.
2. **Investments:** Dividends, interest, and growth from portfolios.
3. **Business Ownership:** Income or proceeds from a business.

Why It Matters:

- It reflects the diverse ways people create financial stability in retirement.
- It encourages building multiple income streams to weather uncertainties.

Action Step:

Assess your stool—are all three legs strong? If not, plan how to reinforce or create new income streams.

The Bucket Plan

What It Is:
A strategy that organizes your money into three buckets based on when you'll need it:

• **Now Bucket:** Immediate needs like your emergency fund and short-term living expenses.

• **Soon Bucket:** Funds to hedge against inflation and provide retirement income in the next 10 years.

• **Later Bucket:** Assets reserved for legacy, long-term care, and growth in the second 10+ years of retirement.

Why It Matters:
• It simplifies saving and spending strategies for each stage of life.
• It ensures your financial plan adapts to your evolving needs.

Action Step:
Work with your advisor to allocate assets into these buckets based on your goals and risk tolerance.

How to Use These Concepts

Take these frameworks and make them your own. Use them to guide meaningful discussions with your financial advisor or to create a personalized strategy. These tools are designed to help you build, grow, and protect your wealth, all while keeping your goals and values front and center.

The goal isn't perfection—it's progress. Let these concepts empower you to take the next step toward financial clarity, confidence, and success.

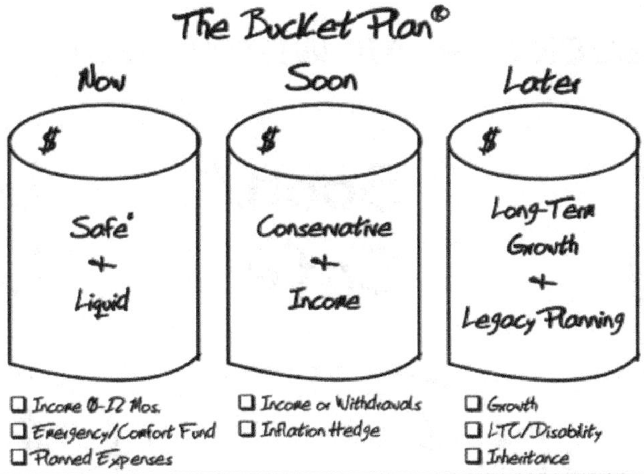

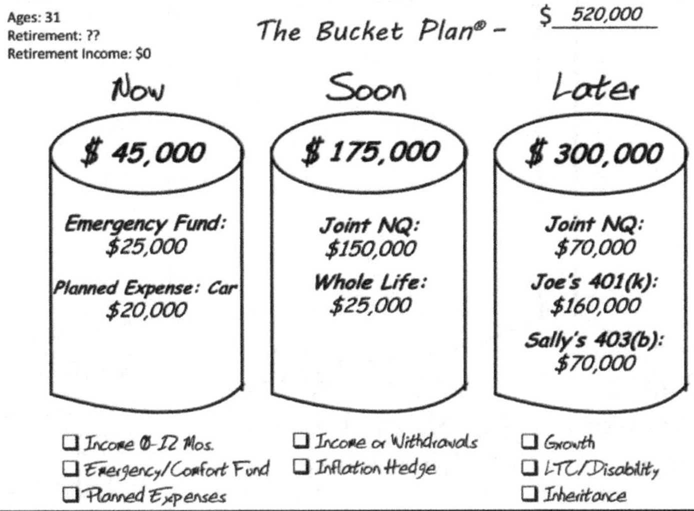

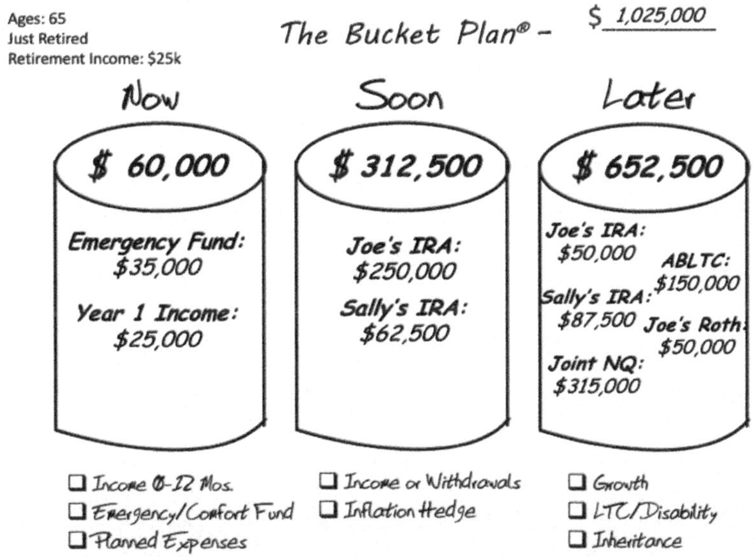

*Disclaimers: *Money referred to as safe in the Now Bucket is intended to mean money held in a bank and subject to FDIC limitations.*

BUCKET PLAN WORKSHEET

Now/ Liquid | **Soon/ Safe** | **Later/ Legacy**

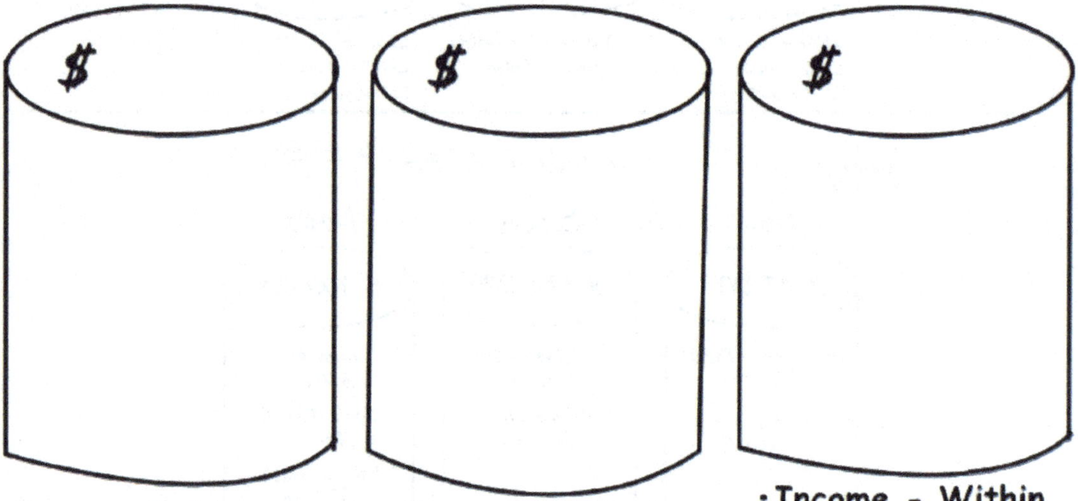

Now/ Liquid
- Income 0-12 mos.
- Emergency/ Comfort
- Planned expenses

Soon/ Safe
- Income - Within the Next 10 Yrs
- Inflation Hedge

Later/ Legacy
- Income - Within the Second 10 Yrs
- LTC/ Life
- Inheritance

MONTHLY RECAP

MONTH OF

THIS MONTH'S ACHIEVEMENTS

WHAT DO YOU FEEL WORKED THIS MONTH?

WHAT DO YOU FEEL DIDN'T WORK THIS MONTH?

THINGS TO DO MORE OF

MONTHLY GRATITUDE

Money TALK$

SMALL BUSINESS BUDGETING *(Bonus Section)*

SECTION TWELVE

MONTHLY PLANNER

MONTH & YEAR

SUN	MON	TUE	WED	THU	FRI	SAT

TO DO:

THIS MONTH'S GOALS

MONTHLY AFFIRMATIONS

POSITIVE AFFIRMATION

I WILL finish the year strong and prepare for a prosperous future.

Money TALK$

Opening Times
OPEN
TRULY INDEPENDENTLY OWNED AND MANAGED

Small Business spending plan & Tracking

Running a small business requires an understanding of key financial terms and effective tools for tracking income, expenses, and profits. This section will define basic financial terms, provide templates for tracking business performance, and offer space for planning financial growth and reinvestment.

Basic Business Terms for Financial Literacy

Revenue: This is the total amount of money generated by your business from selling goods or services before any expenses are deducted. Also known as gross income or sales.

Expenses: These are the costs required to run your business, including rent, utilities, salaries, inventory, marketing, and more.

Net Profit: This is the amount of money left after all business expenses have been deducted from revenue. It is often called the bottom line.

Net Profit = Revenue – Expenses

Cash Flow: This refers to the net amount of cash moving in and out of your business. Positive cash flow means more money is coming in than going out, while negative cash flow means the opposite.

Cost of Goods Sold (COGS): This is the direct cost of producing the goods or services that a business sells. For example, raw materials and labor costs are part of COGS.

Profit Margin: This is a percentage that indicates how much of your revenue is profit. It's calculated as:

Profit Margin=(Net Profit/ Revenue) × 100

Assets: These are things your business owns that have value, such as equipment, inventory, property, or cash.

Liabilities: These are your business's debts or financial obligations, such as loans, accounts payable, or credit card balances.

Use the templates on the next few pages to track your business income, expenses and profit/loss margins.

Money Talk$ Business Income Tracker

DATE	REVENUE SOURCE	AMOUNT
01/01/2025	Product Sales	$3,421.87
		$
		$
		$
		$
		$
		$
		$
		$
		$
		$
	TOTAL REVENUE:	$

Business Expense Tracker

Track every category of expenses your business incurs, from operating costs to one-time expenses.

DATE	EXPENSE CATEGORY	DESCRIPTION	AMOUNT
01/01/2025	Rent	Office Rent	$ 1,250.00/mo
			$
			$
			$
			$
			$
			$
			$
			$
			$
			$
	TOTAL EXPENSES:	$	

Profit & Loss Statement

This statement summarizes your income, expenses, and net profit over a period of time.

MONTH	TOTAL REVENUE	TOTAL EXPENSES	NET PROFIT (LOSS)
JANUARY	$	$	$
FEBRUARY	$	$	$
MARCH	$	$	$
APRIL	$	$	$
MAY	$	$	$
JUNE	$	$	$
JULY	$	$	$
AUGUST	$	$	$
SEPTEMBER	$	$	$
OCTOBER	$	$	$
NOVEMBER	$	$	$
DECEMBER	$	$	$
	ANNUAL TOTAL	$	

Growth & Reinvestment Plan Worksheet

Create a strategy for reinvesting profits to fuel future business growth.

GROWTH STRATEGY	INVESTMENT REQUIRED	EXPECTED RETURN	TIMELINE/ TARGET DATE
Hire 2 Staff	$ 63,000/year	$ $435,000/year	12 Months
	$	$	
	$	$	
	$	$	
	$	$	
	$	$	
	$	$	
	$	$	
	$	$	
	$	$	
	$	$	
	$	$	
	$	$	
	$	$	

MONTHLY RECAP

MONTH OF

THIS MONTH'S ACHIEVEMENTS

WHAT DO YOU FEEL WORKED THIS MONTH?

WHAT DO YOU FEEL DIDN'T WORK THIS MONTH?

THINGS TO DO MORE OF

MONTHLY GRATITUDE

Made in United States
Orlando, FL
05 November 2026

90209470R00118